Words for the Theatre

In *Words for the Theatre*, playwright David Cole pursues a course of dramaturgical self-questioning on the part of a playwright, centred on the act of playwriting.

The book's four essays each offer a dramaturgical perspective on a different aspect of the playwright's practice: How does the playwright juggle the transcriptive and prescriptive aspects of their activity? Does the ultimate performance of a playtext in fact represent something to which all writing aspires? Does the playwright's process of withdrawing to create their text echo a similar process in the theatre more widely? Finally, how can the playwright counter theatre's pervasive leaning towards the 'mistake' of realism?

Suited to playwrights, teachers and higher-level students, this volume of essays offers reflections on the questions that confront every playwright, from an author well-versed in supplying words for the theatre.

David Cole is a playwright who has written two prior books of dramatic theory: *The Theatrical Event* and the Nathan Award-winning *Acting as Reading*. His plays may be found at www.davidcoleplaysandprose.com.

Focus on Dramaturgy
Series Editor: Magda Romanska

The *Focus on Dramaturgy* series from Routledge – developed in collaboration with TheTheatreTimes.com – is devoted to the craft of dramaturgy from multiple contemporary perspectives. This groundbreaking comprehensive series is authored by top professionals in the field, addressing a variety of current hot topics in dramaturgy.

The series is edited by Magda Romanska, an author of the critically-acclaimed *Routledge Companion to Dramaturgy*, dramaturg, writer, theatre scholar, and Editor-in-Chief of TheTheatreTimes.com.

Shakespeare in Three Dimensions
The Dramaturgy of *Macbeth* and *Romeo and Juliet*
Robert Blacker

Words for the Theatre
Four Essays on the Dramatic Text
David Cole

For more information about this series, please visit: www.routledge.com/performance/series/RFOD

Words for the Theatre

Four Essays on the Dramatic Text

David Cole

 Routledge
Taylor & Francis Group

LONDON AND NEW YORK

First published 2019
by Routledge
2 Park Square, Milton Park, Abingdon, Oxon OX14 4RN

and by Routledge
605 Third Avenue, New York, NY 10017

First issued in paperback 2020

Routledge is an imprint of the Taylor & Francis Group, an informa business

British Library Cataloguing-in-Publication Data
A catalogue record for this book is available from the British Library

Library of Congress Cataloging-in-Publication Data
Names: Cole, David, 1941– author.
Title: Words for the theatre.
Description: Abingdon, Oxon ; New York, NY : Routledge, 2019. | Series: Focus on dramaturgy | Includes index.
Identifiers: LCCN 2019011602 | ISBN 9781138240636 (hardback : alk. paper) | ISBN 9781315283173 (ebook)
Subjects: LCSH: Playwriting.
Classification: LCC PN1661 .C559 2019 | DDC 808.2—dc23
LC record available at https://lccn.loc.gov/2019011602

ISBN 13: 978-0-367-72805-2 (pbk)
ISBN 13: 978-1-138-24063-6 (hbk)

Typeset in Times New Roman
by Apex CoVantage, LLC

For Helen and Bert Cole

Contents

Preface: words from a playwright

There are two questions any reader taking up this volume is likely to have:

1   What are these four very different essays doing in the same book?
2   What is a book made up of these four essays doing in a series on dramaturgy?

Fair questions, both; and, it might seem, quite unrelated. But the two questions have a single answer, are in fact two versions of a single question.

I am not a dramaturg. I have neither studied nor taught nor practiced dramaturgy.

I am a playwright, which is to say I have worked closely with dramaturgs from time to time. It is not, however, on the basis of such secondhand experience that I venture to speak out here with a "focus on dramaturgy." On what basis, then?

The time is past (if there ever was such a time) when dramaturgs did no more than conduct historical research for directors and supply program notes. A present-day dramaturg may be called upon to serve as "ideal spectator" or to design lobby displays, to moderate post-show "talkbacks" or to write blog posts.

Doubtless, some of this activity comes near to, or overlaps with, playwriting. Dramaturgs, for example, adapt and revise scripts or, if the production is a communal, unscripted one, lend a hand in the "devising" of its action.

Still, one instinctively feels, whatever else a dramaturg may be or do, he or she *is not the one who writes the thing*. No one would think to proclaim an equivalence between "dramaturg" and "playwright" if the term itself did not proclaim it or at least sanction the claim. For *dramatourgos*, from which "dramaturg" derives, is, as is often noted (though rarely with sufficient astonishment), the ancient Greek word not for "ideal spectator" or "literary adviser" but for "playwright."

This might be deemed an outworn or incidental connection, had it not found its way into one after another modern European language. In French, Spanish and Portuguese, in Russian and Polish, some form of "dramaturg" is the word for "playwright" and some form of "dramaturgy" the word for "playwriting." So far as I know, Toby Cole's 1961 anthology *Playwrights on Playwriting* (containing essays by Ibsen, Chekhov, Pirandello, etc.) has never been translated into French, but, if it were, the title would read: *Les Dramaturges sur la Dramaturgie.*

We need not be slaves to etymology, but neither let us be too proud to take a hint. The hint being . . . what, exactly? That playwrights are "really" dramaturgs (or dramaturgs, playwrights)?

That every playwright should serve as, or at least strive to get in touch with, his or her own "inner dramaturg"?

No, rather, it is a matter of recognizing that some degree of dramaturgical musing comes with the territory of being a *dramatourgos*, a playwright. Certainly, the two figures who did most to establish dramaturgy as both concept and practice were working playwrights: Lessing (the author of *Nathan the Wise* as well as *The Hamburg Dramaturgy*) and Brecht.

I am also a playwright, and the issues that these four essays explore are, I would hold, issues with which playwrights inevitably deal, whether or not they go on to offer, as I now shall, an account of their dealings.

Let me try to suggest how each of the essays that follow may best be read as the reflections of a *dramaturge sur la dramaturgie*, a playwright on playwriting.

Essay I

To write a play is to produce two objects utterly unlike yet impossible to tell apart.

A theatre script is both the transcript of prior, fictive exchanges (the incidents of the play) and a prescription for subsequent, actual exchanges (rehearsals/performances of the script).

The problem is that, distinct as these transcriptive and prescriptive projects sound (and are), each issues in the same words: the text of the play. "Stay, illusion" both *transcribes* what Horatio said to the Ghost "that night" on the battlements and *prescribes* what the actor playing Horatio will say to the actor playing the Ghost tonight at 8:20.

To be a playwright is thus to be engaged in two sharply different activities, which, however, since both generate a single, self-identical text, there seems no way of distinguishing.

This is a dilemma so familiar as to pass unnoticed, yet once one begins to notice it, profoundly strange.

In ESSAY I, I begin to notice it.

Essay II

Should a playwright ask, "What is it that distinguishes my enterprise from that of other writers?" one answer immediately suggests itself: the playwright alone produces a text whose true nature, whose eventual future, is to be an event: rehearsal/performance of that very text.

There are, however, any number of authors and critics who maintain that a poem "must be thought of as an event in time," that a story "is not the narration of an event but that event itself" – that, in short, *all* texts are events ("the text is an event," "a literary work . . . is always also an event").[1]

And specifically, we are time and again assured that works of (nondramatic) literature are *theatre* events, in which "language acts, 'performs'," sentences "talk to each other as . . . speakers do in drama" and "prose performs a pantomime" – a claim borne out with startling literalness when, in certain novels, the narrative prose suddenly "breaks into script" for a stretch (Joyce, Melville) or simply becomes a script (Cormac McCarthy, Faulkner).

Thus, the very thing that seemed to distinguish the playwright from other writers (and playwriting from other kinds of writing) stands revealed as an ambition on the part of all writing – why this should be so I will try to suggest – which the playwright does not so much uniquely entertain as enact on behalf of all.

Essay III

They go out for drinks; you go home to rewrite. They go on to their next gig; you go back to your desk. . . .

Playwrights are no more solitary than other writers – writing is solitude – but they are more likely to have their solitude brought home to them by the nature of the institution on whose behalf they incur it.

Theatre is the most public of arts, transacted among persons, before persons, in some shared civic space. To write a play is, at least for a time, to draw apart from all this. But here is the surprising thing: just such a tendency toward withdrawal may be discerned in theatre itself.

One indication of this is the startling readiness of writers of every sort to employ "theatre" as a metaphor for internal experience. Poets, psychologists, theologians, critics – all speak of "mental performances" of "inner dramas" presented on "inner stages" in "the theatre of the private mind."

More direct evidence of such indrawing on theatre's part is the profusion of inner spaces and internalizing practices in actual theatre work: backstage, offstage, green rooms, dressing rooms; subtexts, closed rehearsals, inner life of character, working from the outside in. . . . Plainly, theatre has an affinity for the inside, *has* an inside, *wants to go in* – and the playwright goes in after it.

Or maybe it is theatre that goes in after the playwright.

For, we shall find, what theatre ultimately goes on to be is even such a text as the playwright first went apart from it to produce.

Essay IV

Essays I–III address the concerns of any playwright, of playwriting as such. Essay IV is addressed specifically (though not exclusively) to playwrights in the English-speaking theatre. For Essay IV treats of realism, its sorrows and limitations, and to write plays in English is to be forever feeling a pressure toward realism.

My own sympathies lie, and have always lain, far from realistic drama. I tend to favor Claudel over O'Neill, Genet over Mamet, Adrienne Kennedy over Wendy Wasserstein, and, within the oeuvre of a single playwright, the less over the more realistic works – *The Ghost Sonata*, say, over *Miss Julie*. And the "postdramatic theatre" chronicled by Hans-Thies Lehmann – the productions of Robert Wilson, Richard Foreman, the Wooster Group, The Mabou Mines, etc. – has consistently meant more to me *as a playwright* than the boulevard drama on offer against it uptown.

All this, I long assumed, was only a matter of personal preference. But realism, I have come to see, is not merely a less rich or less capable mode of theatre but a *mistake* about theatre, or maybe a mistake about art to which theatre, as the art that represents events by other events, is especially prone.

Realist art is often faulted for its semiotic naiveté or political complacency. Such critiques, whatever their merits, approach realism from without. The problem I see is with realism's own ambitions for itself, with what one might call *the internal contradictions of realism*.

The more stringently realist art attempts to give us the thing itself, the more frankly it proclaims itself to be this attempt – and so the more plainly it assumes the character of that ironic self-mirroring that is at the farthest remove from realism.

Theatre, because its medium is event, can make the strongest claim of any art to be offering the thing itself – only an actor can represent eating a carrot by eating a carrot – and so finds itself utterly enmeshed in that play of ironies from which realism fancies itself to have escaped, to be, indeed, the escape.

Meanwhile, the pressure on every English-speaking playwright to slip the actors their carrots is unremitting.

***

These four will not be every playwright's questions (though they are, I maintain, questions that confront every playwright). But surely the posing of such questions by a playwright should occasion no surprise. Dramaturgy, claims its root, is a going apart to muse upon the practice of the *dramatourgos*; and who more given to such musings than the *dramatourgos* himself or herself?

To be sure, not every playwright will choose to "go apart" in the company of Mallarmé, Boccaccio, Hume, the poststructuralists . . . it is a rather personal constellation. But its being so follows from the kind of book this is. *Words for the Theatre* recounts one playwright's journey toward dramaturgical self-awareness. It does not attempt – would, indeed, depart from its purpose in attempting – any sort of survey or synthesis of current scholarship. For the most part, only those texts and productions that spurred me to, or helped me along on, my journey as I pursued it find a place in this account. Other, later works, whatever their intrinsic merits, receive less attention.

Thinking about the problems of playwriting may be deemed too narrow a definition of dramaturgy in a theatre where dramaturgs also rear lobby displays, host talkbacks, build websites. . . . But thinking about the problems of playwriting is not too narrow a definition of dramaturgy *for a dramatourgos*. *Words for the Theatre* contains the reflections of one accustomed to supply words for the theatre.

Note

1 Phrases cited in passing here will be fully annotated at the appropriate point in the Essays proper.

Acknowledgments

I am grateful to the following friends and colleagues for sustenance and critique: Marya Bradley, Garrett Dell, Kristen Ebert-Wagner, Elinor Fuchs, Don Gertmenian, Meg Gertmenian, Elizabeth Gilliam, Kenneth Gross, Amie Keddy, Ben Letzler, Kenneth Letzler, Robert Letzler, John Leubsdorf and Kelly Matera.

Magda Romanska helped me to see this book for the book it is.

I am thankful to and for my wife, Susan Letzler Cole, true reader and true love.

Essay I   The dramatic text as transcript and prescription

— Baba, why are texts intended for use in the theatre called "scripts"?
— Attend.

The script as transcript

Occasionally, one comes upon a theatre script that incorporates stretches of transcript. Plays about Joan of Arc – Shaw's *Saint Joan*, Anouilh's *The Lark*, Irene Fornes' *The Trial of Joan of Arc in a Matter of Faith* – work in the retorts of Joan preserved in the transcripts of her interrogation at Rouen.[1] *Inherit the Wind* includes exchanges from the Scopes trial.[2] In *Execution of Justice*, Emily Mann's 1986 docudrama about the shooting of Harvey Milk, "the words come from trial transcripts, reportage and interviews."[3]

Some theatre scripts are virtually all transcript. *Are You Now or Have You Ever Been* draws its dialogue entirely from the blacklist hearings of the House Un-American Activities Committee.[4] *In the Matter of J. Robert Oppenheimer* is based on the transcript of a government inquiry into Oppenheimer's security clearance.[5] Courtroom transcripts supply the texts of Daniel Berrigan's *The Trial of the Catonsville Nine* (concerning the destruction of draft files)[6] and Peter Weiss's *The Investigation* (concerning Auschwitz).[7] Brigitte Jaques's play *Elvire Jouvet 40* takes as its text a series of seven stenographically transcribed acting classes given by Louis Jouvet in 1940.[8] Anna Deveare Smith's one-woman show *Fire in the Mirror* was drawn word for word from a set of tape-recorded interviews conducted by Smith herself.[9] And *The Trial of Mussolini*, an anonymous 1943 British play by "Cassius," claims to be "a verbatim report" – i.e., a courtroom transcript – of the Italian dictator's war crimes trial.[10]

To be sure, in all these cases the original transcript has been modified: speeches have been selected, abridged, reassigned;[11] extraneous material – monologues, projected quotations, stage directions – has been introduced.[12]

Yet in each instance the text performed in the theatre is recognizably that of an (edited) transcript.

A script composed, in whole or in part, of a transcript would appear to be a rather special case of the dramatic text; and indeed, productions that employ such scripts have long been recognized as constituting a genre of their own: "documentary theatre" or "docudrama," as chronicled by Marvin Carlson in *Shattering Hamlet's Mirror* (2016).

The script of a docudrama must, it would seem, take for its subject matter some real-world event of which, at the time, a transcript was made: the House Un-American Activities Committee hearings; Louis Jouvet's 1940 acting classes; the trial of Mussolini. . . .

Wait, though: Mussolini never came to trial. He was summarily executed on April 28, 1945.[13] This inconvenient fact, which at first seems to remove *The Trial of Mussolini* from the category of transcript-based scripts, in fact suggests how that category may be an ampler one than at first appears.

The Trial of Mussolini claims to have come into being as follows. Someone ("Cassius") is imagined as having been present, pen in hand, at an imagined event, which he faithfully transcribed. "One might suppose that he had stood by at the time and had overheard what passed." "It is as if he had been actually present . . . and had taken down what he heard and saw, . . . looks, words, and gestures, just as they happened." These familiar sentences of Hazlitt's are not, of course, accounts of "Cassius" composing *The Trial of Mussolini* but of Shakespeare at work.[14] To write a play, Hazlitt suggests, is to be imaginatively present to a series of exchanges that one sets down as they occur.

To this way of thinking, a transcript is not a special case of the dramatic text; it is a trope for the dramatic text as such. And a supposed transcript that, like *The Trial of Mussolini* (or *King Lear* or *Rosmersholm*), turns out to be merely a fiction is a trope for the dramatic fiction as such. For while dramatic fictions are many, the fiction of the dramatic text is always this: an exchange has been transcribed. Theatre may imitate all manner of actions, but what the dramatic text is always pretending to be is a transcript.

I do not think, and I do not think Hazlitt meant to imply, that the playwright necessarily *experiences* playwriting as transcription.[15] Yet even with this proviso, the image may seem a confining one. All that following-about and setting-down sounds like a recipe for the merest realism. Certainly the one playwright I know of who actually spoke of his work in these terms – George Kelly, who subtitled his 1924 comedy *The Show-Off* "A Transcript of Life in Three Acts" – meant by this to suggest that his play was true to life.[16] And Peter Brook's electronic update of Hazlitt – "imagine," he advises the actor, "that someone . . . followed [your character] everywhere with a tape recorder"[17] – no more than literally describes the work method of hyperrealist playwright Anna Deveare Smith, trailing after her interview subjects with a tape recorder so as eventually to replicate their transcribed speech, stutter by stutter, onstage.[18]

Of course, in fact neither Kelly nor Brook nor Smith is in any simple sense a realist. And it is well to recall that the fictive events which a playwright may be imagined as present to and setting down need scarcely be realistic ones: one may as soon "follow around" three witches as three sisters, as readily record the exchanges of Classical Walpurgis Night as those of *'Night, Mother.*

Still, the trope seems to impose limits, if not on the actions a script may represent, yet on the questions a script might seek to raise concerning its own act of representation. What prior utterance may such unspeechtagged speeches as the following be taken as transcribing?

> This piece is a prologue. It is not the prologue to another piece but the prologue to what you did, what you are doing, and what you will do. You are the topic. This piece is the prologue to . . . your actions.
>
> (Peter Handke, *Offending the Audience*)[19]

> A landscape neither quite steppe nor savannah, the sky a Prussian blue, two colossal clouds float in it as though held together by wires, or some other structure that can't be determined, the larger one on the left might be an inflated rubber animal from an amusement park that has broken away from its mooring, or a chunk of Antarctica floating home. . . .
>
> (Heiner Müller, *Explosion of a Memory/Description of a Place*)[20]

Offending the Audience and *Explosion of a Memory* make hard cases of the script as transcript. But the *concept* of the script as transcript helps them make their hard case. *Who speaks, and to whom? What manner of exchange is here set down?* – such are the very questions these innovative plays sought, for once, to put in play.

No, if there is any problem with conceiving the theatre script as fictive transcript, it is not that this view excludes unconventional or experimental plays but, rather, that it may fail to exclude certain other, nontheatrical texts that no less display the character of fictive transcripts but are plainly not scripts. One thinks first of the Platonic dialogues and the long line of "transcribed" philosophical discussions to which these gave rise: St. Anselm, Berkeley and Hume all subsequently offered their philosophical musings in dialogue,[21] as did Tasso, Dryden and Valéry their musings on art.[22] The so-called "Melian Dialogue," in which Thucydides imagined the citizens of Melos pleading stichomythically with the Athenians for their lives, is a fictive transcript starting up off the pages of a work of history.[23] The Talmud abounds in transcripts of conversations known to be imaginary because the supposed participants lived in different eras[24] – as did, of course, the speakers in Walter Savage Landor's *Imaginary Conversations* (e.g., Seneca and Epictetus).[25] And then, there is the whole tradition of "closet drama," that vast corpus of texts for all the world scriptlike, transcriptlike, but, for all that, not scripts.

Of course, in practice we feel pretty confident we know how to distinguish all such pretenders from actual plays: they are "not dramatic," "not meant for the stage," etc. But these are highly relative, not to say question-begging, terms. The "Melian Dialogue" seems to me more dramatic than the Trojan Council scene (II.i) from *Troilus and Cressida*: does it therefore seem to me a script?[26] Plato's dialogues were never intended to be staged but occasionally have been: do they, then, turn out to have been scripts all along?[27] Wordsworth's *The Borderers* has struck most readers as the very type of a closet drama, yet in fact it was submitted to Covent Garden – and turned down.[28] Had the decision gone otherwise, would we have been mischaracterizing a theatre script?

I do not know the answer to any of these questions, but I know what follows from their being unanswerable. Hazlitt's image of the playwright as on-the-scene transcriber ("it is as if he had been actually present . . . and had taken down what he heard and saw") does not, it appears, uniquely characterize the writer of *plays*. (Indeed, at least one novelist has described his writing practice in these terms: "it is a pity," laments Henry James of a conversation he felt bound to omit from *The Tragic Muse*, "that so little of this rich colloquy may be *transcribed* here.")[29] Simply to offer a fictive transcript is not yet to have offered the theatre a script. What more than a transcript must a theatre script offer?

Some hint of a reply may be sought in the conventions that attend, or once attended, the writing of stage directions.

The script as prescription

Stage directions are customarily written in the present tense. (*Exit, pursued by a bear. The street door is slammed shut below. They do not move.*) Their being so reflects a basic truth about the dramatic text: that because its events can at any moment be made present (by enactment), those events must in some sense be going on "now."[30]

So familiar is this convention, and so grounded in the nature of theatre scripts themselves, that it comes as rather a shock to learn that the practice is far from universal. From the early middle ages through about 1590,[31] a stage direction, whether given in English or (as tends to be the case in medieval play manuscripts) in Latin, while occasionally making use of the present tense, far more often employed either the *future*:[32]

> Here shall they leave off and dance around the cross.[33]
> Here shall they be served with wine and spices.[34]
> Here shall Simeon bear Jesus in his arms.[35]

or the so-called *jussive* (= "commanding") *subjunctive*:[36]

> Then let Herod . . . inflamed with rage, fling down the book.[37]
> Let young Marius chase Pompey over the stage.[38]
> Here let him quake and stir.[39]

In Latin, these future and subjunctive forms look alike and, what is more, frequently appear side by side in the same stage direction:

> *Tunc . . .* **veniet** *Jesus stans in medio discipulorum, ac postea* **dicat**:
> (Then . . . Jesus **shall come,** standing in the midst of his disciples, and afterward, **let him say**:)[40]

The convergence is suggestive. For in Latin as in English, the emphatic future ("Thou shalt not kill") and the jussive subjunctive ("Let there be light") both have the force of imperatives, which is to say, both enjoin subsequent action. Employed in a stage direction, each instructs the actor what to say and do *next*:

> Cain, like a madman, shall rush upon Abel wishing to kill him and shall say to him:[41]
> Then he shall take the book, and, astonished, he shall say:[42]
> Then let the midwives, seeing the Magi, say:[43]

Such constructions may strike the modern reader as over-deliberate or quaint. But if our present-day, present tense stage directions pick up something essential about the dramatic text – namely, that it is where the play's events are "always happening" – so also do the more forward-looking stage directions of medieval drama, namely, that a script is a set of instructions for what you must say or do "in the future," i.e., in the hour of rehearsal and performance. If, as we have seen, a dramatic text professes to be the transcript of some earlier exchange (between characters), no less does it offer itself as a prescription for subsequent exchanges (between actors).

Of course, no more than "transcript" does "prescription" by itself provide an adequate account of a theatre script. Yes, scripts prescribe events. But, just as not every text that claims to transcribe a prior exchange finds a place in the theatre (recall those philosophical dialogues, imaginary conversations, etc.), so neither does every action-prescribing text prescribe action to the stage. You will not come upon these prescriptive words from *The Book of Common Prayer*:

> Then, while the earth shall be cast upon the Body by some standing by, the Minister shall say,[44]

nor these, from the owner's manual of a 1958 Crosley refrigerator:

> Pry out the two screw hole plug buttons on the bottom left side of the top door and lower door. Remove the door stops (metal plates) on the bottom of each door and install them on opposite sides.

in the "Drama" section of your local library.

Clearly a dramatic text is *both* transcript and prescription, but as standing in what relation to each other? That is the crucial – and, one may feel, the only interesting – question. For, by themselves, these two terms no more than restate that a theatre script both records and enjoins activity, neither of which is exactly news. What must a text be, what manner of text must this be, that somehow manages at once to represent prior action and to enjoin further representation of the very action it represents?

Brecht, in an acting exercise, and certain Asian theatre traditions as a more general practice, call upon actors to read aloud the stage directions of the scripts they perform. To speak stage directions as dialogue is to treat prescribing words as transcribed words, thus hinting at an equivalence between prescription and transcription themselves. What basis might there be for any such claim of equivalence?

As a first step toward answering this question, allow me to retell a story from Day 3 of *The Decameron*.

The dramatic text as transcript and prescription

A married Lady – "her name I shan't tell you," demurs Boccaccio's narrator, "because it would give offense to certain people who are still alive"[45] – is in love with a Galant but has no safe means of communicating with him. When, however, she learns that her would-be lover is friends with a certain Friar-confessor, she hits on a ploy. Every day she recounts to the Friar, under the guise of the latest "outrage" the Galant has offered her, the very move she wishes him to make next. With the result that each morning the Friar, supposing that he upbraids his friend's most recent transgression, unwittingly gives him his marching orders for that night. So, for example, the Lady's indignant "I can't show my face at the window without his popping up before me" conveys *Present yourself tonight at my window.* "He climbed a tree in our garden and was about to enter my room" means *You can reach my bedroom via a tree in the yard.* And so forth.

In this ploy of Boccaccio's Lady, we may see an image of the dramatic text as *at once* transcript and prescription.

The account the Lady gives the Friar of the words she and her Galant have (supposedly) already exchanged is what we have found a theatre script to be: a fictive transcript. The instructions the Galant receives from the Friar as to what words and actions he and the Lady shall perform next are no less what we have found a theatre script to be: a set of prescriptions.

"Yes, but" (suppose we ungraciously pressed the Lady) "which is it *really*, this ploy of yours: the transcribing of a prior fictional, or the prescribing of a subsequent actual, interchange?" The Lady would be at a loss how to reply. She would have failed to understand the question because she would have failed to understand the distinction.

It is a question, and a distinction, that theatre also fails to understand and that a text shows itself to be for the theatre by failing to understand. The dramatic text is always undecidably transcript and prescription.[46]

The script as rescript

By what name might we call the dramatic text thus understood as at once, indistinguishably, transcript of some prior, and prescription of some subsequent, course of events?

There is a term from Roman law, not perhaps a perfect fit but pointing in the right direction: "rescript." Rescripts were rulings issued by emperors in response to inquiries from their subjects, in which the emperor recorded his sense of the situation and decreed its outcome.[47]

These legal documents thus displayed what we have found to be the two basic aspects of a dramatic text. On the one hand, a rescript offered a representation of the situation as that situation presented itself to the emperor[48] – i.e., offered a "transcript" of its author's vision of events.[49] On the other hand, a rescript supplied instructions as to how those events, so envisioned, must now play out – i.e., offered a prescription by its author to its recipients of the actions they were to perform.[50]

In theory, a rescript was merely a legal opinion, "advice, not an order."[51] Since, however, this "advice" was coming from the most powerful man on earth, in practice "rescripts amounted to a form of authoritative interpretation"[52] through which "the emperor exercised untrammelled power."[53] (In later eras, popes, kings and czars were all much given to issuing rescripts.)[54]

Thus, not only does a rescript display the same two aspects – transcriptive and prescriptive – as a dramatic text but, like a dramatic text, presents them as indistinguishable. *Your will is my command* must be the response of one offered such a document, not out of blind deference but merely in recognition of the kind of document one has been offered, namely, a text in which there is no distance, no distinguishing, between the imagined event transcribed in, and the actual event prescribed by, it.

If I now propose that we bring over this Roman legal term to designate play texts, it is scarcely because I regard their authors as little Caesars. Not the playwright's will, but the identity of transcriptive and prescriptive intent in whatever he or she wills, is inarguable. A theatre script, like a rescript, does not know how to say what kind of text it is – whether "truly" or "chiefly" or "finally" transcript or prescription – and its drawing a blank on this point it the very thing that marks it as a text for the theatre.

***

    – But, Baba, why are texts intended for use in the theatre called "scripts"?
    – "Script" is short for "rescript."

Notes

1 So, for example (one of many), the following exchange from Joan's trial transcript:

> Asked if she knew whether she were in the grace of God,
> She answered: If I am not, may God put me there; if I am, May He keep me there.

(*The Trial of Joan of Arc*, trans. W. S. Scott [Evesham: Arthur James, 1996], 56) reappears, more or less unaltered, in several of the dramatic texts based on it. (Pace Hans-Thies Lehmann and Peter Szondi, I do not, as a rule, employ "drama" or "dramatic" in the special senses conferred upon these terms by those authors in, respectively, *Postdramatic Theater* [London: Routledge, 2006], 21–22 and *Theory of the Modern Drama* [Minneapolis: University of Minnesota Press, 1987], 5–6).

2 Jerome Lawrence and Robert E. Lee, *Inherit the Wind* (New York: Random House, 2007). "Only a handful of phrases have been taken from the actual transcript of the famous Scopes trial," declare the authors in their prefatory note, xi.

3 This account of the sources of Mann's dialogue appeared in the program for the 1986 New York production of *Execution of Justice* at the Virginia Theatre (*Playbill*, vol. 86, no. 3 [March 10, 1986]: 29).

4 Playwright Eric Bentley affirms that he "used a record published by the United States government, and most of the testimony drawn upon can be found in . . . my own volume *Thirty Years of Treason*" (Eric Bentley, *Are You Now or Have You Ever Been and Other Plays* [New York: Grove Press, 1977], 4). According to its subtitle, *Thirty Years of Treason* (New York: Viking, 1971) contains

"excerpts from hearings before the House Committee on Un-American Activities, 1938–1968."

5   Heinar Kipphardt, *In the Matter of J. Robert Oppenheimer*, trans. Ruth Speirs (New York: Hill and Wang, 1968), 5.

6   Daniel Berrigan, *The Trial of the Catonsville Nine* (Boston: Beacon Press, 1970), 7.

7   Peter Weiss, *The Investigation*, trans. Jon Swan and Ulu Grosbard (New York: Pocket Books, 1967), ix.

8   Brigitte Jaques, *Elvire Jouvet 40*, trans. Albert Bermel (Purchase, NY: Pepsico Summerfare, 1988), i–ii.

9   Greg Tate, "Bewitching the Other," *Village Voice* (July 21, 1992): 101.

10 "Cassius," *The Trial of Mussolini* (London: Gollancz, 1943). The phrase "verbatim report" occurs in the subtitle: "Being a Verbatim Report of the First Great Trial for War Criminals held in London in 1944 or 1945." Normally, in accounts of "docudramas," one would carefully distinguish between productions that employ pre-existing transcripts to be their scripts and productions (like Anna Deveare Smith's) where a transcript is only first taken so as to serve as script. For present purposes, however, only the distinction between scripts based on actual transcripts and scripts (such as *The Trial of Mussolini*) "only pretending" to be transcripts need concern us.

11 **Selected:** Compare the list of witness-characters on p. 8 of Bentley, *Are You Now* with the fuller witness list in Bentley, *Thirty Years*, xi–xiv. **Abridged:** The script of Kipphardt, *Oppenheimer* is about 125 pages long. "The record of the hearings ran to some 3,000 typewritten pages," 115. **Reassigned:** "The nine witnesses sum up what hundreds expressed" (Weiss, *Investigation*, ix). The only transcript-based production I know that retains every single word of the transcript it uses is *Arguendo*, in which the experimental company Elevator Repair Service "stages . . . in its entirety . . . the oral arguments of a 1991 [Supreme Court] case centered on a statute requiring exotic dancers to wear G-strings." See the review by Alexis Soloski, *Village Voice* (September 25–October 1, 2013): 22.

12 **Added monologues:** See Kipphardt, *Oppenheimer*, 6, 25–26, 31–32, 38–39, 42–43. **Projected quotations:** See Berrigan, *Catonsville Nine*, 24–25, 33–35, 46–47, 49, etc. **Stage directions:** A number of these have been inserted in all the transcript-based scripts cited in Essay I, notes 4–8.

13 John Gooch, "Bunga Bunga" (review of two studies of Mussolini's diaries), *TLS* (October 14, 2011): 22.

14 The first sentence appears in Hazlitt's 1814 review of Kean as Hamlet (William Hazlitt, "A View of the English Stage," in *Complete Works*, ed. P. P. Howe [London: Dent, 1930], vol. 5, p. 185). The second sentence is from the *Julius Caesar* chapter of his 1817 book *Characters of Shakespear's Plays* (*Complete Works*, vol. 4, p. 197). I have always felt that Hazlitt's fondness for this image of the playwright as on-the-scene transcriber of witnessed exchanges must owe something to his 1812–13 stint as a parliamentary reporter for the *Morning Chronicle* (see Herschel Baker, *William Hazlitt* [Cambridge, MA: Harvard University Press, 1962], 192–193 and Nikki Hessell, *Literary Authors, Parliamentary Reporters* [Cambridge, UK: Cambridge University Press, 2012], xx–xxi, 97–128). Such a connection appears less likely, however, when one reflects that (1) Hazlitt found the quality of the parliamentary exchanges he transcribed distinctly sub-Shakespearean (see his essay "On the Present State of Parliamentary Eloquence,"

in *Complete Works*, vol. 17, pp. 5–21) and (2) he did not literally transcribe them, but rather produced a "mixture of full reportage, summary, omission and reconstruction from memory" (Hessell, *Parliamentary Reporters*, 167).

15 Such, however, is certainly the experience of the playwright character "Shakespear" in Shaw's *Dark Lady of the Sonnets*, who rushes about the stage noting down the contributions to his complete works which his fellow-characters seem unable to stop uttering – a joke that perhaps owes something to Hazlitt's image of the playwright as everpresent transcriber. See David Cole, *Acting as Reading* (Ann Arbor: The University of Michigan Press, 1992), 246.

16 Edith Oliver, "At Long Last Love" (review of a 1992 New York revival of *The Show-Off*), *New Yorker* (November 16, 1992): 125.

17 Quoted in John Lahr, "Hamlet Minceur" (review of Brook's 2000 Paris production of *Hamlet*), *New Yorker* (December 18, 2000): 100.

18 See Essay I, n. 9.

19 In *Kaspar and Other Plays*, trans. Michael Roloff (New York: Farrar, Straus and Giroux, 1971), 28.

20 In *Explosion of a Memory: Writings*, ed. and trans. Carl Weber (New York: PAJ Publications, 1989), 97.

21 St. Anselm, *Cur Deus Homo* (1099); George Berkeley, *Three Dialogues Between Hylas and Philonus* (1713); David Hume, *Dialogues Concerning Natural Religion* (1776). The introductory remarks of Hume's speaker Pamphilus provide what is still probably the best defense of dialogue as a medium for speculative thought. For the theatrical potential of philosophical, and especially Platonic, dialogues, see Martin Puchner, *The Drama of Ideas* (Oxford: Oxford University Press, 2010), 11–15, 121. Puchner, indeed, argues (73) that the whole self-reflexive, metatheatrical turn in modern theatre finds its prototype in Plato's dialogues.

22 Torquato Tasso, *Minturno, or On Beauty* (1593–94); John Dryden, *Essay on Dramatic Poesie* (1668); Paul Valéry, *Dance and the Soul* (1921), *Eupalinos, or The Architect* (1921).

23 Thucydides, *The Peloponnesian War*, Book 5, sections 85–113 in *The Landmark Thucydides*, ed. Robert B. Strassler (New York: Simon & Schuster, 1996), 351–356.

24 David Kraemer, *The Mind of the Talmud* (New York: Oxford University Press, 1990), 5–7, 82–83, 85–90, 109.

25 Walter Savage Landor, *Imaginary Conversations* (London: Henry Coburn, 1828), vol. 3, pp. 493–502.

26 "Comedy, tragedy . . . are obvious generic influences" on the Melian dialogue, according to Simon Hornblower, *A Commentary on Thucydides* (Oxford: Oxford University Press, 2008), vol. 3, p. 219.

27 Hornblower, *Commentary*, 220 and refs. there.

28 Mary Moorman, *William Wordsworth: The Early Years, 1770–1803* (London: Oxford University Press, 1968), 350–351. Beyond all such borderline cases, the whole nineteenth century tendency to identify "true" theatre with inner theatre and inner theatre with solitary reading works against any absolute distinction between closet and staged drama. I discuss this matter further in Essay III, pp. 42–43.

29 Henry James, *The Tragic Muse* (Harmondsworth: Penguin, 1978), chap. 23, p. 264 (italics added).

30 See David Cole, *The Theatrical Event* (Middletown: Wesleyan University Press, 1975), 8 and *Acting as Reading*, 77.

31 See Linda McJannet, *The Voice of Elizabethan Stage Directions* (Newark: University of Delaware Press, 1999), 176–177 and Alan C. Dessen and Leslie Thomson, *A Dictionary of Stage Directions in English Drama, 1580–1642* (Cambridge, UK: Cambridge University Press, 1999), entry: *let*, 131.

32 McJannet, *Voice*, 113.

33 Quoted in Alan J. Fletcher, "The N-Town Plays," in *The Cambridge Companion to Medieval English Theatre*, ed. Richard Beadle (Cambridge, UK: Cambridge University Press, 1994), 179.

34 *Mary Magdalene* (Digby), l. 113sd, in David Bevington, ed., *Medieval Drama* (Boston: Houghton Mifflin, 1975), 693.

35 *Killing of the Children* (Digby), l. 484sd, cited in McJannet, *Voice*, 59.

36 See McJannet, *Voice*, 113 and James B. Greenough and J. H. Allen, *New Latin Grammar* (Boston: Ginn, 1903), 278–279.

37 *The Service for Representing Herod* (Fleury), l. 58sd, in Bevington, *Medieval Drama*, 63.

38 Thomas Lodge, *The Wounds of Civil War* (1588), ll. 333–334, cited in Dessen, *Dictionary*, entry: *let*, 131.

39 Thomas Preston, *Cambises* (1584), l. 1165sd, cited in McJannet, *Voice*, 114.

40 *Christ Appears to the Disciples* (Chester), l. 168sd, in Bevington, *Medieval Drama*, 633.

41 *The Service for Representing Adam*, l. 678sd, in Bevington, *Medieval Drama*, 109.

42 *The Purification* (Chester), l. 55sd, in Peter Happé, ed., *English Mystery Plays* (Harmondsworth: Penguin, 1979), 321; translation: 673 note 6.

43 *The Service for Representing Herod* (Fleury), l. 90sd, in Bevington, *Medieval Drama*, 65.

44 "Burial of the Dead," in *The Book of Common Prayer* (Greenwich, CT: The Seabury Press, 1953), 333.

45 Giovanni Boccaccio, *The Decameron*, trans. Guido Waldman (Oxford: Oxford University Press, 1993), Day III, Tale 3, pp. 181–190.

46 "Undecidably" may appear an overstatement; after all, the transcriptive and prescriptive moments of a dramatic text seem distinct enough. "Stay, illusion" *transcribes* what Horatio said to the Ghost "that night" on the battlements and *prescribes* what the actor playing Horatio shall say to the actor playing the Ghost tonight at 8:20. What, however, becomes of this commonsense distinction in the case of "Millbrook," Part 3 of the Wooster Group's 1984 production *L. S. D. (. . . Just the High Points . . .)*? In performance, "Millbrook" gave the impression of a semi-improvised, druggy cast party, with the actors staggering, giggling, and calling out isolated lines from *The Crucible*, a speeded-up version of which they had just performed. But this impression was quite misleading. In fact, "Millbrook" had come about as follows. The Group earlier rehearsed *The Crucible* on acid, videotaped the rehearsal, and now recreated live in the theatre every lurch, giggle and cry preserved on the tape. One may argue that this was a *sui generis* experiment. Still, it was a *sui generis* experiment made possible by the readiness of the same material to pass from *transcript* (of *The Crucible*'s exchanges) to *prescription* (of *The Crucible*'s enactment) to *further transcription* (the videotaped rehearsal) that now *prescribed* further action ("Millbrook") to be performed by those whose prior enactment of this very material it had come into being by initially *transcribing*. It does not seem excessive to find here some evidence for the indistinguishability of the transcriptive and prescriptive aspects

of the dramatic text. (The above account of the origins of "Millbrook" was supplied by Norman Frisch, the *L. S. D.* dramaturg, in a post-performance conversation on October 20, 1984. Frisch's account is confirmed by Wooster Group director Elizabeth LeCompte in David Savran, *The Wooster Group, 1975–1985: Breaking the Rules* [Ann Arbor: UMI Research Press, 1986], 195–196.)

47 Tony Honoré, *Emperors and Lawyers*, 2nd edition (Oxford: Clarendon Press, 1994), vii.

48 Ibid., 46, 59.

49 In fact, rescripts were often literally transcripts, taken down by a secretary, of the emperor's orally delivered decisions. Ibid., 43.

50 Like the prescriptive medieval Latin stage directions discussed above, rescripts often employed the future tense with imperative force, e.g., *praeses provinciae curabit* ("the governor will see to it [that]"). Ibid., 49.

51 Ibid., 40.

52 Ibid., 41.

53 Ibid., 6.

54 **Popes:** See *The Oxford Universal Dictionary*, 3rd edition, rev. and ed. C. T. Onions (Oxford: Oxford University Press, 1955), entry: *rescript*, def. 1a., p. 1712. **Kings:** See *A Rescript of H. M. the King of Prussia to Mr. D'Andrie, His Minister at the British Court* (London: J. Osborne, 1744). **Czars:** See Constance Garnett's translation of Leo Tolstoy, *War and Peace* (New York: Random House, 1956), 189, 571, 873.

Essay II   The dramatic text as type of the text

The Theatre of God's Judgments, The Theatre of Genealogies, Theatre of Cities, Theatrum Orbis Terrarum . . .

One cannot read very widely in or about early modern literature without coming upon book title after book title of this sort.

The Theatre of Fine Devices, Theatrum Vitae Humanae, Theatrum Mundi, Universae Naturae Theatrum . . .

None of these volumes are about theatre or contain plays. Some are works of philosophy or theology; others treat architecture, genealogy, geography, emblems . . . *The Theatre for Voluptuous Worldlings* is a poetry anthology; *The Theatre of Love*, a collection of novels. *Theatrum Sanitas* is a medical handbook; *Theatrum Chemicum*, a compilation of writings on alchemy. What can have led all these authors of treatises and compilers of anthologies to call their books "theatres"?

One may feel one grasps, in a general sort of way, the logic of this practice. Books, after all, are "performances" designed to attract an "audience"; to publish is to bring a "production" before the "public," etc.

Still, the trend is puzzling. For one thing, the experience of ploughing through these (mostly) weighty tomes cannot have been very much like theatregoing.[1] Nor was this an era (if there has ever been such an era) when associating one's intellectual or artistic project with theatre was likely to raise it in anyone's esteem. To early modern taste, epic poetry represented the height of literary attainment; theatre – profane, vernacular, urban – was far down the list of cultural splendors, if it so much as made the list. We may view the sixteenth and seventeenth centuries in Spain, France and England as a golden age of theatre. But it was no less a golden age of hostility toward theatre. Indeed, while medieval attacks on the stage were far from rare, one must go back to the Church Fathers[2] to find anything like the sustained torrent of abuse that greets us in the sixteenth and seventeenth centuries.[3] The "antitheatrical prejudice" so characteristic of the period was no doubt shared by more than a few of the sober scholars who titled their books "Theatre" or "Théâtre" or "Theatrum" of this or that. Why, then, did they so title them?

For a long time, I made small headway on this problem, until one day I chanced on a sentence by Paul de Man that seems to bear no relation to it:

> We have, to a large extent, lost interest in the actual event that Mallarmé was describing as a crisis, but we have not at all lost interest in a text that pretends to designate a crisis when it is, in fact, itself the crisis to which it refers.[4]

De Man is here contrasting the slight intrinsic interest possessed by the subject matter of an essay of Mallarmé's (certain minor advances in French prosody) as compared with the imaginative force displayed by the essay ("Crise de vers") itself. Nothing could be farther from de Man's mind than the use of "theatre" in book titles. Yet the terms in which he frames his contrast – "a text that pretends to designate a crisis when it is, in fact, itself the crisis to which it refers" – begin to suggest what may be at stake in such titling.

The text as event

How can a text be a "crisis"? For that, it would have to be even such an "actual event" as de Man here *opposes* to mere texts; for what is a crisis but a certain kind of – a decisive, a culminating – event? Can texts be events?

Indeed they can, critics of every stripe hasten to assure us. "The text is an event," proclaim, in identical words, the deconstructionist William Spanos and the reader-response critic Stanley Fish[5] – an "open event," adds Wolfgang Iser,[6] and therefore to be "experienced as an event."[7] "Texts as Events" an historian calls his essay on historical documents, for such "texts are events and make history."[8] "Books as Events" is the subtitle of a Folger Institute seminar that explores "how [seventeenth century] political books . . . were understood as deeds."[9]

As these last two examples illustrate, it is not only texts in general but specific kinds of texts that may bear this character. "The poem . . . must be thought of as an event in time," asserts Louise Rosenblatt (in an essay entitled "The Poem as Event").[10] "Poems are dialectical events," claims Harold Bloom[11] – a claim that Paul Alpers perhaps only seems to reverse in proposing that "the 'gross events' of [Spenser's] *Faerie Queene* . . . are . . . lines and stanzas of poetry."[12] And much the same claim has been advanced for prose fiction by Maurice Blanchot: "The tale is not the narration of an event, but that event itself."[13]

It is not hard to see what underlies this manner of speaking. After all, everything that can happen to a text, or that a text can make happen, is some kind of event. The conceiving, imagining and elaborating of a text are (mental) events. The writing and revising of a text are events. Publication is an event. Once published, the text may make a splash, stir controversy, or possibly sink without a trace – events all. Above all, "the reading of a text is an event."[14] Surely all these many events attendant upon the text must impart something of their event-status to the text itself? Surely the text itself can be no less of an event than all the events that produce, or are produced by, it?

But this makes no sense. The analytic philosophers have taught us to regard events as "changes in objects."[15] Doubtless, as between objects and the changes they undergo there are some middle cases. If I fix my gaze on a just-applied dab of cadmium yellow, am I looking at some still-wet pigment (an object) or watching paint dry (an event)? But there seems little doubt which side of the object/event divide texts must be placed on. Much as one might like to think (and I shall speak presently of why one might like to think it) that a text is "not an object . . . but an act that is also an event"[16] or at very least is "suspended between object and event,"[17] plainly a text is some kind of entity there before one. As complex, as dynamic, as elusive an entity as you please, but . . . a thing in the world, something in your path. "A thing, they say, is an event," muses Robert Frost, but concludes: "Not quite."[18] Such was long since the verdict of Clement Greenberg on his rival Harold Rosenberg's attempt to claim event-status for abstract expressionist paintings (surely one of the sources for the subsequent literary trend to claim it for texts). What appears on these canvases, Rosenberg held, is "not a picture but an event." No, countered Greenberg, merely "the . . . aftermath of an event"; for, as Mary McCarthy pointed out, you can't hang an event on the wall.[19]

Nor can you slip one between the covers of a book. Mallarmé's essay (to return to our Paul de Man passage) cannot in fact *be* the crisis it pretends to designate, though the writing, reading, and reception of it may all be crises and are certainly events.

All this seems too plain to argue with. Surely what we have here is not a false position that cries out to be refuted but a true need that cries out to be understood. It is a need that lets itself be glimpsed in such claims as the following:

Sometimes a book is itself an event and not only a record of events.[20]

and declares itself openly in a formulation like this:

Even when a literary work is a representation of something else it is always also an event in itself.[21]

Not only a record . . . a representation of something else – do we not here catch an echo of writing's perennial (or at least post-Platonic) unease with its own secondariness, its status as mere recounting, retelling, writing up? Must we not recognize, in all this talk of the text as an event like any other, the latest vocabulary for art's longstanding aspiration to be no mere mimesis ("not only a record") of reality but a reality among other realities, a force or act or presence in the world, "part of the res itself and not about it"?[22]

This is, one might suppose, an aspiration plainly destined for defeat, since texts are not events.

But wait: there is one kind of text that, while no more an event than the others, "has a future" as an event: the dramatic text. Your paperback of *King Lear* is as little a happening or occurrence – a "change in an object" – as your paperback of *Tom Jones*. But one day, at the hour it is rehearsed or performed, it shall occur as an event, namely, a rehearsal or performance of *King Lear*.

The dramatic text thus represents the best hope of a text turning out to be, after all, "an event in the life of the reader."[23]

How, then, if *all* texts were, in some sense, "dramatic" texts – were theatre-in-waiting, so to speak? *But they're not!* common sense wants to protest. Try telling that to the authors of all those "theatre"-titled volumes that were our starting point. For only now are we in a position to grasp the true nature of the claim being advanced by such titles. If your book on architecture or geography or medicine is a "theatre," then it is possible to see it as, potentially, an event in the world, since theatre texts are – or at length shall be – events in the world.

But the tendency to speak of nondramatic texts as "theatre," and thus as (eventual) events, goes well beyond this late-Renaissance titling practice; it is, in fact, ubiquitous. If we have come on a fair number of claims that texts are events, we encounter a virtual torrent of claims that texts are *theatre* events.

The text as theatre event

> [R]egardless of author, I adored the works in the Hetzel series [of children's books], little theatres whose red cover with gold tassels represented the curtain; the gilt edges were the footlights.[24]

This boyish fancy of Jean-Paul Sartre's (realized, to some degree, in present-day children's "pop-up" books) has been shared by any number of adult readers.

That a text is "a . . . script to guide performance"[25] (since "[r]eading a work . . . makes it happen")[26] is a commonplace of poststructuralist criticism.

But for many contemporary critics, as for the young Sartre, texts are not just scripts to be realized in the theatre of reading; they are *themselves* "theatre." We must, we are told, think of "the text as theatre,"[27] as "a staging of the linguistic event,"[28] as "another scene, on another stage . . . in the unfolding of the play of writing,"[29] as a "dramatic representation upon the stage of discourse."[30]

On this textual stage "language acts, 'performs'."[31] Sentences "talk to each other as . . . speakers do in drama."[32] A text's very words play parts ("functions, in traditional syntax, are but roles played by words")[33] – and not necessarily speaking parts: Rabelais's writing "performs a pantomime of its own autonomy and productivity";[34] Robert Walser's short prose pieces are "little dancers who dance . . . until they are completely spent."[35] In short, to read a book is to have before one some variety of "the text as spectacle,"[36] to witness "sophisticated verbal performances that are certainly events."[37]

And if, as we saw earlier,[38] it is not only the text as such but particular kinds of texts – poetry, fiction – that may be regarded as "events," no less often shall we find poems and novels spoken of as *theatre* events. "I look upon a poem as a performance," declares Robert Frost.[39] If it be objected that the performance in question is not necessarily a theatrical one, no such doubt attaches to the claim of one critic of the *Aeneid* that "Virgil's epic poem is in effect a theater in which the words *mime* the gestures."[40]

Such imagery has an up-to-date ring. But the ancient Roman poet Martial long since described his poetry as "my theatre" (*theatrum meum*).[41] And indeed, modern-sounding critical formulations of the poem as theatre event often turn out to have a long pre-modern history. It may be a contemporary critic, Thomas Greene, who writes that Joachim du Bellay's sixteenth century sonnet sequence *Les Antiquitez de Rome* "watches itself act out the conventional humanist rituals and sets ironic traps for its performance."[42] But another sixteenth century sonnet sequence, Sidney's *Astrophil and Stella*, is described in its own Preface as a "theater of pleasure . . . a proper stage" where "the comedy of love is performed by starlight."[43] And, of course, Shakespeare famously "equates his books of poetry with a [performed] play" in Sonnet 23: "O, let my books be then the . . . /dumb presagers of my speaking breast,"[44] a "dumb presager" being one who mimes an action in advance.

No less than critics of poetry, commentators on fiction seem eager to claim for the texts they study the status of theatre events. Thus, if Robert Frost proposed to "look upon a poem as a performance,"[45] *The Novel as Performance* is the title given to a 1986 study of experimental fiction.[46] Henry James may have regarded an acted play as "a novel intensified,"[47] but in the view of certain later writers, fiction is theatre *tout court*; for do not story-tellers "make a theatre of their tale-tellings"?[48] Thus, according to one contemporary critic, in Defoe "the text is a stage and all its characters are players";[49] while another holds that "[a]nyone who opens one of Dickens's novels" must be "prepared to enter a 'theatre'," and accordingly titles his study *The Dickens Theatre*.[50]

What the words know

It is fair to ask whether all these many assertions that texts of every sort "are theatre" add up to anything. Granted that a considerable number of writers speak in this manner, are we looking at anything more than a manner of speaking?

That here is no casual comparison but a deeply felt (or hoped) equivalence seems underwritten by language itself:

> I have often thought, that I should certainly have been as successful on the boards as I have been between them.[51]

The thing that makes this *mot* of Dickens possible – the fact that "boards," in English, happens to mean both "stage" and "book cover" – might seem the merest coincidence, did not some version of this pun reappear in language after language in era after era.

Already in classical Latin the word for "story" or "tale" (*fabula*) is also the word for "play" or "drama."[52] But it is in the Latin of the middle ages that words meaning both "text" and "theatre," "text *as* theatre," proliferate. A twelfth century dictionary assigns to *scaena* the senses of both "theatre" and "script."[53] We are likely to know the word *mansio* ("mansion") as "a term for [one of] the 'houses' marking particular locations on a medieval . . . stage"; but *mansio* also appears in the titles of late medieval encyclopedias, where it designates the book itself.[54] Perhaps the most striking instance of a Latin word pointing in both these directions occurs in a fifteenth-century will, where among the possessions of the deceased is listed the manuscript of "a certain play . . . comprising six *paginae*." *Paginae* is the common Latin noun for "pages." But it is also the usual term for the successive "pageants" of a cycle drama.[55] A page, the language itself seems to insist, is already a performance; the dramatic text, a theatre event – not, perhaps, a very surprising identification in a culture that regarded its theatre productions as "quick [= living] books."[56]

Double meanings of this sort are scarcely confined to the middle ages or to Latin. The stage/page duality we noted in *scaena* survives in its modern English cognate: we, too, refer to both a "scene change" and "the last scene of Act IV." In French, one speaks of *mise-en-scène* (the mounting of a theatre production) and *mise-en-page* (the arrangement of graphic elements on a page).[57] The use of the *mise-en* . . . construction in both contexts implies a close parallel, if not identity, between the disposing of elements on a page and onstage.

But the clearest example in French of the language itself claiming for books the status of theatre events is the French word *théâtre* itself. In some contexts *théâtre* has the same semantic range as English "theatre": *Theatre and Its Double* exactly translates *Le théâtre et son double*. There is, however, another use of the word without parallel in English. My volume of translated plays by Marivaux is called: Marivaux, *Plays*.[58] My volume of plays by Montherlant in the original French is titled: Montherlant, *Théâtre*.[59] Grotowski deplored this usage, seeing in it a mark of the inveterate literariness of French theatre, printed scripts being, after all, "not theatre but dramatic literature."[60] This seems to me to get things exactly backwards. To identify the collected scripts of Montherlant as (already!) the "*théâtre*" of Montherlant – what is this but to claim for the dramatic text the status of a theatre event, to recognize the "quick book" of performance as already in progress in the book itself?

Breaking into script

More persuasive than all such designating – whether by individual authors or by language itself – of texts as "theatre" would be some actual instances of nondramatic texts that display the characteristics of a theatre script or event. Do we find such instances?

Actually, we have already found some. The claim of theatre status asserted by all those early modern "theatre"/"*theatrum*"/"*théâtre*" book titles we started with did not always stop at the title. Ortelius's 1570 map collection *Theatrum Orbis Terrarum* featured a frontispiece "arched and framed in columns and ringed with allegorical figures [that] recalled the theatrical scene."[61] Nor is this an isolated instance: "baroque theatre architecture was crucial to the aesthetics of the baroque title page."[62] And Theodor Zwinger's *Theatrum Vitae Humanae* (1565) takes things well beyond the title page. It "opens with a 'Proscenia' . . . describes its readers as spectators, its words as actors"[63] – the whole book is a show. It is, moreover, a show "divided into Acts and Scenes,"[64] and in this recalls a far more celebrated sixteenth century book/theatre.

In 1580 Sir Philip Sidney completed the first version of *The Countess of Pembroke's Arcadia*, the so-called *Old Arcadia*. The genre of this immense production is scarcely in doubt. A tale of disguised princes pursuing their amours through a (literally) arcadian landscape of shepherds and country lasses, the *Old Arcadia* is a vast pastoral romance in prose with interpolated verse "eclogues" marking the divisions between its five sections.

It is therefore somewhat startling to find these five sections of narrative prose titled as follows:

The First Book or Act of the Countess of Pembroke's
    Arcadia
The Second Book or Act
The Third Book or Act
The Fourth Book or Act
The Last Book or Act[65]

The *Old Arcadia* is by no stretch a play. None of its source or predecessor texts – "a third-century Greek romance, a medieval 'French' book of chivalry, and an early sixteenth century Italian pastoral"[66] – are plays. Why, then, "Book *or Act*"? Scholars explain the choice of "book" as an homage to Chaucer's *Troilus and Criseyde*, also in five books, which Sidney is known to have admired.[67] "Act" may likewise reflect an admiration of Sidney's, perhaps for Sackville and Norton's five-act tragedy *Gorboduc*[68] or possibly for the five-phase "Terentian structure of exposition, action, complication, reversal and catastrophe."[69] But the really interesting word here is "or": "Book *or* Act." This is not the exclusionary "or" of "your money or your life!" It is, rather, the "or" of felt equivalence between (only apparent) alternatives, as in *Twelfth Night, or* – as you may just as well like to call it – *What You Will*.

How did these seemingly quite distinct alternatives – segment of a narrative, section of a play – come to be regarded by Sidney as interchangeable? Perhaps the equivalence was suggested to him by the double meaning of the Latin word *fabula* noted above:[70] "narrative" *and* "play." (Sidney was an accomplished Latinist.) At any rate, the claim he makes for the *Old Arcadia* is the very claim we found inscribed in that Latin word: to be a true "book" is to be an "act," i.e., an event, and specifically a *theatre* event, since it is theatre texts – scripts in acts – that may rise to the level of events when theatre rises to perform them.

The only other early modern book I know that is, like Sidney's and Zwinger's, divided into "acts" – "6, 7, 8, 9, each containing up to twenty scenes . . . with Prologue, Chorus and Catastrophe"[71] – is Thomas Prynne's huge *antitheatrical* tract, *Histriomastix* (1633). The intent of this running irony may well have been "to turn the terminology of dramatic structure against its usual practitioners."[72] But such an appropriation is also an acknowledgment of theatre's power, being itself an event, to shape events. Antitheatricalism fights theatre with theatre; the antitheatricalist text fights theatre by becoming a dramatic text.

Any claim of script or theatre status for the discursive, slow-moving *Old Arcadia* may appear forced. In the case of another, present-day *fabula*,

Cormac McCarthy's *The Sunset Limited*, Sidney's "book or act" equivalence is experienced by the reader as well as asserted by the author in his subtitle, "A Novel in Dramatic Form."

The Sunset Limited depicts a single long conversation between a suicidal white college professor and an evangelical black ex-con who has snatched him out of the path of an oncoming subway train and now seeks to talk some Christian sense into him. What concerns us is its mode of depiction.

The text of *The Sunset Limited* is visibly "in dramatic form," consisting as it does entirely of dialogue between its two characters, speech-tagged "White" and "Black," together with the occasional italicized stage direction, e.g., *A door to the outer hallway and another presumably to a bedroom.*[73] *He adjusts his glasses.*[74]

From moment to moment, one feels one is reading a script (and in fact *The Sunset Limited* has been twice presented onstage).[75] Setting down the book, however, one feels one has come to the end of a novel, albeit one with the now-in-progress quality of a theatre script. All told, it has been all event.

The *Old Arcadia* and *The Sunset Limited*, to the extent that they announce themselves to be in "acts" or "in Dramatic Form," lay claim to "theatre" status from the first. But there are other novels – *Moby-Dick, Ulysses, Requiem for a Nun* – that, beginning in a mode clearly (if complexly) narrative, at some point along the way develop into something like a theatre script. Moments of this sort, when a nondramatic text as it were "breaks into script" (on the analogy of "breaking into song"), are of particular interest to us as figuring *within* a text that text's aspiration to break forth as (stage) event.

For example, in Chapter 40 of *Moby-Dick*,[76] after some 250 pages of narrative prose, we suddenly find ourselves reading a play ("Midnight, Forecastle"), over the brief course of which the *Pequod*'s crew sing, dance, muse, trade barbs and fantasies, and at length spring into action against a rising squall.

Moby-Dick experiments with one after another manner of telling. Its prose plays at being now that of a sermon (Chapter 9), now that of a zoological treatise (Chapter 32, "Cetology"), now that of a philosophical essay (Chapter 42, "The Whiteness of the Whale"). But only for these 8 or 9 pages does it play at being a play. Other chapters depicting the actions and interactions of the *Pequod*'s crew (e.g., Chapter 48, "The First Lowering") go forward in narrative prose. Why does theatre "break out" just here?

That we are about to witness an outbreak of *some* sort is hinted at, in the pages just preceding Chapter 40, by gathering images of, well, *outbreak*:

[t]he chick that's in him pecks the shell. 'Twill soon out.

(Chapter 36, p. 258)

How can the prisoner reach outside except by thrusting through the wall?

(Chapter 36, p. 262)

That the coming outbreak will be of *theatre* is likewise foreshadowed by the steady accumulation of script conventions – specifically, soliloquies and stage directions – in this not-yet-dramatic text. Chapters 37, 38 and 39 are soliloquies delivered by the *Pequod*'s captain, first mate and second mate, respectively. And each soliloquy is introduced by a stage direction:

The cabin; by the stern windows; Ahab sitting alone and gazing out

(Chapter 37, p. 265)

By the Mainmast; Starbuck leaning against it

(Chapter 38, p. 267)

Stubb solus, and mending a brace

(Chapter 39, p. 268)[77]

It is no coincidence that the first such stage direction – (*Enter Ahab: Then, all*) – occurs in Chapter 36 (p. 257). For it is in Chapter 36 that Ahab first declares the true object of the *Pequod*'s voyage – and thus, the true action of the novel: to find and kill Moby Dick, the white whale that has taken off Ahab's leg some years earlier. It is at this moment when the action first shows its true character that it begins to show the character of theatre.

Only, as yet, *begins* to show it: for it is not until all the "actors" – i.e., the *Pequod*'s full crew – have been assigned their "roles" in Ahab's drama and agreed to perform them, that the curtain can go up. This "casting" of the crew is accomplished by the end of Chapter 36, when Ahab nails to the mast a gold dubloon and proclaims it will go to whichever sailor first sights Moby Dick. "The crew, man, the crew! Are they not one and all with Ahab in this matter?" (p. 262), muses the captain – and soon enough has his answer: "we are the lads to hunt him up his whale" (p. 274). *Enter Ahab: Then, all.* Whereupon, all its roles now cast, "*Foresail rises and discovers*" (p. 269) . . . the "show" in progress. At the moment when, at length, the *full reality* of the text's central event breaks upon those who must perform it, the text itself, as if in acknowledgment, "breaks into" script, a script being the one sort of text whose events may look forward to becoming, at length, fully real.

When theatre "breaks out" in the "Nighttown" section of James Joyce's *Ulysses*, the outbreak is on quite another scale than Melville's "Midnight, Forecastle" playlet. Not for a single brief chapter but for nearly a quarter of its 750-page length, *Ulysses* becomes a script – a script, moreover, that (with some tweaking) can be, and actually has been, performed onstage.[78]

But the contrast between Melville's and Joyce's mid-novel dramas goes beyond length or stageability. The events dramatized in *Moby-Dick*, Chapter 40 are on the same level, of the same order, as those narrated elsewhere in *Moby-Dick*: the sort of thing, we readily believe, likely to occur in such a milieu at such a juncture. The same can be said of the pre-"Nighttown" events of *Ulysses*, which, for all the obliqueness of their telling, are famously those of an ordinary June day in 1904 Dublin: a funeral, a walk on the beach, business transacted, meals consumed. . . .

At first, the events of "Nighttown" also display this everyday character: An older man (Bloom) and a younger (Stephen) wander through their city's red-light district, encountering whores, bawds, soldiers, etc. But soon incidents of a very different order begin to occur. Characters not physically present – Bloom's wife,[79] daughter (p. 530), and old flame (p. 435) – appear. The dead – Paddy Dignam, whose funeral Bloom attended that morning (p. 463), Bloom's father (p. 430), William Shakespeare (p. 553) – appear. Physical objects – the bar of soap that Bloom earlier purchased for his wife Molly, a fan belonging to whoremistress Bella Cohen – spout verse and engage in dialogue (pp. 433, 515–16). Mythic figures – a nymph from the picture hanging in the Blooms' bedroom (p. 532), "Reuben J. Antichrist, wandering Jew" (p. 495) – arrive on the scene. At length such sequences of events as the following take the stage:

> *Bloom . . . passes through several walls, climbs Nelson's Pillar . . . bids the tide turn back and eclipses the sun by extending his little finger*
> (p. 485)

I have said that these sorts of things do not occur earlier in the novel. But in a sense they do: they occur *to Bloom*, as fantasies, recollections, etc. For example, from early on Bloom's long-dead son Rudy has been "appearing" in his thoughts: "he would be eleven now if he had lived" (p. 66), "I could have helped him on in life" (p. 88). Now, in "Nighttown":

> (*Against the dark wall a figure appears slowly, a fairy boy of eleven. . . .*)

Bloom

(*Wonderstruck, calls inaudibly.*)
  Rudy!

(p. 593)

All along it has been the method of *Ulysses* that whatever enters Bloom's (or Stephen's) mind enters the novel; what is different here is that now whatever enters Bloom's mind enters the novel *as an event*:

Bloom

O, I so want to be a mother.
   (*Bloom . . . bears eight male yellow and white children*)

(p. 484)

This may seem a new representational mode for *Ulysses*, but it would be truer to see it as a new degree of explicitness about what has been *Ulysses*' mode of representing from the first. Throughout, it has been the premise of this "stream of consciousness" narrative that its inner "events" are as much events as its external occurrences. And precisely this is conveyed by such inner events beginning to occur "onstage" now. Once again, a hitherto nondramatic text's "breaking into script" registers that text's claim of event-status for its representations, a script being precisely a text with a claim to be, after all, an event.

At first glance, William Faulkner's *Requiem for a Nun* does not seem to fit the pattern of a prose narrative "breaking into" script. For (with the big exception of the lengthy prose musings that precede each of its three acts) it is script all along – a full-length play.

But *Requiem for a Nun* (1951) is the sequel to an earlier novel of Faulkner's, *Sanctuary* (1931). In *Sanctuary*, college student Temple Drake is abducted, violated, and consigned to a Memphis brothel by the gangster, Popeye. In *Requiem for a Nun*, Temple, now married and a mother, lives out the consequences and comes to see the meaning of those earlier events. Taking the original all-prose novel and its (almost) all-script sequel together as a single work, we may say that *Sanctuary* does indeed "break into" script – and the script it "breaks into" is *Requiem for a Nun*. And, as is also the case with *Moby-Dick* and *Ulysses*, it is at the moment when Faulkner's text brings forward its principal event that it begins to do its bringing forward in the mode of event, i.e., turns to theatre.

To a far greater extent than *Ulysses in Nighttown*, *Requiem for a Nun* has had an actual life in the theatre. Within a decade of publication it had drawn the attention of such eminent adapter/directors as Erwin Piscator, Albert Camus and Tony Richardson and been produced in six different cities in five countries.[80]

This is all very surprising. True, longtime Mississippi friends insisted that "the thing Faulkner wanted to do most in the world was write a play";[81] true also that he had dabbled in playwriting and theatre criticism while at college.[82] Still, prior to *Requiem for a Nun* he had published no plays and, indeed, claimed to have attended theatre only five times in his life.[83]

He also claimed that *Requiem for a Nun*, at least in its original published form, was "not . . . a play," but rather "some kind of novel" or perhaps "a story told in seven play-scenes inside a novel"[84] – a "*roman dialogué*," as Albert Camus, his French translator/director, put it.[85]

And yet . . . there it stands: three acts of speech-tagged dialogue with stage directions, giving rise to production after production for this theatre-averse novelist.

If pressed, Faulkner would explain that he had written *Requiem* as a script because he had promised his actress friend, Ruth Ford, a play.[86] I propose that the real reason for *Sanctuary*'s sequel taking dramatic form must be sought in *Sanctuary* itself, specifically, in *Sanctuary*'s failure to culminate in a true event.

Sanctuary ends with two murder trials in which justice is not done. *Requiem for a Nun* depicts the effort to reverse the outcome of a third murder trial in which again, arguably, justice is not done – and yet the cycle is broken.

In *Sanctuary*'s first murder trial[87] Lee Goodwin is wrongly convicted and executed (lynched, actually) on the perjured testimony of a false witness, Temple Drake, who, for reasons that never become fully clear, is seeking to protect her rapist/abductor Popeye, the actual killer. In *Sanctuary*'s second murder trial[88] Popeye himself is wrongly convicted and executed on the perjured testimony of an anonymous false witness. As if the ironic link between these two trials were not plain enough, Faulkner lets slip no chance to hammer it home: e.g., "they arrested him [Popeye] for killing a man in one town and at an hour when he was in another town killing somebody else."[89] Or again: At Lee Goodwin's trial, "[t]he jury was out eight minutes";[90] at Popeye's trial, "[t]he jury was out eight minutes."[91] Much as one might like to view Trial Two as *righting* the injustice of Trial One (this time Popeye is punished), all too plainly it achieves this result only by *repeating* the injustice of Trial One (once again the wrong man is punished).

Culminating as it does in this self-cancelling sequence, *Sanctuary* achieves no real outcome: Temple Drake is whisked off to Europe, where she is last glimpsed yawning through a band concert in the Luxembourg Gardens.[92] To accord Temple and her novel some truer resolution, Faulkner continues the story in the play or play-like *Requiem for a Nun*.

Requiem also focuses on a murder trial: that of Temple's black nanny, Nancy Mannigoe, who (it is now several years later) has murdered Temple's infant daughter to "spare" her the degradation of being dragged along on Temple's future sexual escapades. Nancy's trial, however, is not the true action of *Requiem for a Nun*, which begins just after the delivered verdict and ends just before the scheduled execution. The true action of *Requiem for a Nun* is the "trial" of Temple Drake herself before the Governor, whom Temple seeks out in the middle of the night, ostensibly to grant a commutation of Nancy's death sentence but actually to hear her own confession. She confesses to a specific crime (the perjured testimony that got Lee Goodwin lynched)[93] but more basically she confesses to the truth of her nature ("Temple Drake liked evil"),[94] which, she feels, as much as Popeye's brutal actions, set in motion the train of events that will bring Nancy to the gallows.

Nancy's sentence, as Temple well knows, will not be commuted as a result of Temple's last-minute intervention. Nothing comes of Temple's confession; *it* comes:

Temple

What we came here and waked you up at two o'clock in the morning for is just to give Temple Drake a good fair honest chance to suffer.[95]

And its coming – the onset of that "good fair honest chance to suffer" here in the sequel to *Sanctuary* – is the true event to which *Sanctuary* itself, caught in its play of self-mirroring ironies, could never rise. In the end a true event comes to pass, and this is marked by Faulkner's text now, in *Requiem for a Nun*, "breaking into" script, a script being even that form of text whose events shall in the end (in the theatre) come to pass.

My ultimate (in every sense) example of a nondramatic text claiming to be a theatre event labors under the disadvantage of having never been written – although, since it never could have been written, this is less of a drawback than might be supposed.

As the central figure of an active literary circle, Mallarmé was well aware that of the making of books there is no end; and indeed, he made a fair number of them himself. Nevertheless, over time he came to feel it was implicit in the very idea of a book that, ultimately, there could be but *one* of them (*il n'y en a qu'un*)[96] and he actually set about to produce this singleton – *le Livre* (definite article, capital L), as he liked to call it[97] – though predictably never getting much beyond the "notes toward" stage.[98]

Of what would this book to end all books, if ever achieved, have consisted? A poem or poems, one might assume, Mallarmé being a poet and "the Orphic explanation of the earth" being one of the few explicit characterizations he ever gave of his project.[99] But among the 200 or so extant pages of fragments for *le Livre*, we find few if any fragments of poetry.[100] What we do find are long lists of specifications for a five-year cycle of 90-minute readings to be performed in a salon under electric light by a single "*opérateur*" who would deliver to an audience of 24 spectators (each of whom had paid 1,000 francs admission) selections from a text laid out in 20 480-page loose-leaf volumes.[101] Mallarmé lavished much thought on the relation of these various parameters to one another: what, for example, should be the ratio between audience size and number of sheets read? between the number of sessions and the physical dimensions of the loose-leaf binders?[102] Etc.

Based on page after page of this sort of thing, Mallarmé scholars are forever pointing out that the textual and performance aspects of *le Livre* are "translations of"[103] or "inhabited by"[104] each other. But since in fact there exist few traces of *le Livre* apart from these performance specifications – "no 'content' . . . only a series of . . . 'operations'"[105] – it seems truer to say that *le Livre* "would apparently have been a sort of theatrical occasion,"[106] in short, an "*événement*," an event.[107]

The events as which *Moby-Dick* and *Requiem for a Nun* break out when they break into script are events in the action of those novels: Ahab's proclamation, Temple's "trial." Mallarmé's *Livre* does not merely break into some event or other; it offers its own breaking-into-event as its sole, its inevitable, action. And, since *le Livre* claims for itself the status of "only book ever" (*il n'y en a qu'un*), the implication is that a text's – *any* text's – outbreak as theatre event somehow represents literature's sole, inevitable trajectory. What relation between literature and theatre is implied by this extraordinary claim and, indeed, by the whole tendency we have traced to view (literary) texts as (theatre) events?

What is theatre for literature?

What does literature ask or need or want from theatre?

Time and again in these pages I have found myself speaking about writing of a nondramatic sort. I began by noting the presence of "theatre" in the titles of nontheatrical books, went on to analyze the use of theatre metaphors in nontheatrical contexts, and have lately been concerned with the eruption of scriptlike passages in novels. This may already be enough about nondramatic literature for some readers of an essay in dramatic theory.

Yet *what is theatre for literature?* seems to me the question to which our whole inquiry has been leading up, if only because it is the question to which theatre itself inescapably leads back.

For all that, it may not appear a very promising question; for do not the two most familiar ways of thinking about the literature–theatre relation both preclude asking it?

On the traditional view, theatre cannot be "for" literature because it already *is* (a branch or genre of) literature: dramatic literature. On the Artaud-Grotowski view, theatre cannot be "for" literature because it is *against* – or at least, set over against – literature as literature's (mythic, scenic, gestural) "other."

I should like to propose a relation between literature and theatre that looks beyond this tired polarity; or rather, I have already proposed it. I have said that texts "long" to be events.[108] I have shown that in theatre that longing is fulfilled,[109] since a staged script cannot help but be all those event-like things – present, active, voiced – that, away from theatre, a text (as the post-structuralists taught us) can only dream of being. And therefore, I have argued,[110] all texts aspire to the condition of the dramatic text; for a dramatic text goes the way they would all go: toward event.

Of course, in current "postdramatic" theatre work (as H.-T. Lehmann has named it), we come upon more, and more complex, relations between texts and events than the traditional *event realizes text*. Richard Schechner, for example, paradoxically conflates the two in his concept of the "performance text," by which Schechner means "everything that takes place on stage that a spectator experiences."[111]

For the most part, though, theatre continues to cherish for its texts the very aspiration that nondramatic literary texts cherish for themselves. And it is in light of this shared objective that our present question – what is theatre for literature? – may now be answered. The relation between literature and theatre is that of literature to its own aspiring.

If I am asked who exactly is doing the aspiring, I confess to being a little at a loss. I certainly don't mean to suggest that what poets or novelists "really" want to do is write plays (how would I know?) Nor do I wish to imply (though we have seen some evidence of this) that certain nondramatic literary forms are "evolving" toward drama: my point is not an historical one at all. Perhaps, of several unsatisfactory ways of putting it, the least unsatisfactory is this:

> *Theatre is the realization of a hope, the*
> *fulfillment of an ambition, already*
> *entertained by literature for literature*
> *at a moment when there was as yet,*
> *on literature's part, no thought of*
> *theatre.*

Notes

1 It is possible that the word "theatre" in a sixteenth-century book title may, for contemporary learned readers, have evoked images not of their own actual theatregoing but of a (somewhat misconceived?) Greek or Roman stage.
2 Mary H. Marshall, "*Theatre* in the Middle Ages: Evidence From Dictionaries and Glosses, II," *Symposium* 4, no. 2 (November 1950): 378.

3 Rosemary Woolf, *The English Mystery Plays* (Berkeley: University of California Press, 1972), 77.

4 Paul de Man, "Criticism and Crisis," in *Blindness and Insight* (New York: Oxford University Press, 1971), 7.

5 William V. Spanos, quoted in Vincent B. Leitch, *Deconstructive Criticism* (New York: Columbia University Press, 1983), 80; Stanley Fish, quoted in Una Chaudhuri, "The Spectator in Drama / Drama in the Spectator," *Modern Drama* 27, no. 3 (September 1984): 282.

6 Wolfgang Iser, *The Act of Reading* (Baltimore: Johns Hopkins University Press, 1978), 70.

7 Charles Altieri, "The Hermeneutics of Literary Indeterminacy," *New Literary History* 10, no. 1 (Autumn 1978): 91.

8 J. G. A. Pocock, "Texts as Events: Reflections on the History of Political Thought," in *Politics of Discourse: The Literature and History of Seventeenth Century England*, ed. Kevin Sharpe and Steven N. Zwicker (Berkeley: University of California Press, 1987), 29.

9 "A Presse Full of Pamphlets: Books as Events, 1637–1660," seminar directed by Michael Mendle, *Folger Institute Newsletter* 18 (Summer 1994): 1.

10 Louise M. Rosenblatt, "The Poem as Event," in *The Reader, the Text, the Poem* (Carbondale: Southern Illinois University Press, 1978), 12.

11 Harold Bloom, *Kabbalah and Criticism* (New York: Seabury, 1975), 106.

12 Paul J. Alpers, *The Poetry of the Faerie Queene* (Princeton: Princeton University Press, 1967), 36. The phrase "gross events" is Northrop Frye's.

13 Maurice Blanchot, "The Song of the Sirens," in *The Gaze of Orpheus* (Barrytown: Station Hill, 1981), 109.

14 Rosenblatt, "Poem as Event," 20. See also Iser, "reading itself 'happens' like an event" (*Act of Reading*, 68) and Derek Attridge on "the *eventness* of . . . reading" (*The Singularity of Literature* [New York: Routledge, 2004], 136).

15 Brian Lawrence Lombard, *Events* (London: Routledge & Kegan Paul, 1986), ix. The speculations of recent continental philosophers are more hospitable to a view of texts as events. See, for example, Martin Puchner's remarks on Alain Badiou in *Drama of Ideas*, 185–192.

16 Attridge, *Singularity of Literature*, 105.

17 Terry Eagleton, *The Event of Literature* (New Haven: Yale University Press, 2012), 190.

18 Robert Frost, *Selected Prose* (New York: Macmillan, 1968), 38.

19 For a good, brief account of this controversy, see Patrick McCaughey, "Events on Canvas," *TLS* (June 20, 2008): 17.

20 Anonymous review of Michael A. Meyer, *Response to Modernity: A History of the Reform Movement in Judaism* (New York: Oxford University Press, 1988), *Choice* 26, no. 7 (March 1989): np.

21 Anthony Julius, *Trials of the Diaspora: A History of Anti-Semitism in England* (Oxford: Oxford University Press, 2010), 151.

22 Wallace Stevens, "An Ordinary Evening in New Haven," XII, 2, in *Collected Poems* (New York: Knopf, 1969), 473.

23 Rosenblatt, "Poem as Event," 16. A minor character in Stendhal likewise claims that "a good book is an event in my life." (Stendhal [Marie Henri Beyle], *The Red and the Black*, trans. C. K. Scott Moncrieff [New York: Random House, 1953], vol. 2, chap. 31, p. 10).

24 Jean-Paul Sartre, *The Words* (New York: Fawcett, 1964), 46.
25 Altieri, "Hermeneutics," 91.
26 Attridge, *Singularity of Literature*, 87.
27 Phillippe Sollers, quoted in Philip Beitchman, *I Am a Process With No Subject* (Gainesville: University of Florida Press, 1988), 280, n. 8.
28 Attridge, *Singularity of Literature*, 87.
29 Jacques Derrida, *Dissemination* (Chicago: University of Chicago Press, 1981), 142.
30 Frederic Jameson, *The Prison-House of Language* (Princeton: Princeton University Press, 1972), 124. See also David Kornhaber, "Every Text Is a Performance: A Pre-History of Performance Philosophy," *Performance Philosophy* 1 (2015): 24–35. Richard Schechner's semiotic concept of the "performance text" ("all that happens during a performance both onstage and off") sounds similar to, but in fact inverts, both Jameson and Kornhaber. Schechner urges a view, not of the text as event, but of the (performance) event as text. See *Between Theater and Anthropology* (Philadelphia: University of Pennsylvania Press, 1985), 22.
31 Roland Barthes, "The Death of the Author," in *Image-Music-Text* (New York: Hill and Wang, 1982), 143.
32 Robert Frost, quoted in Richard Poirier, "Green Giant," *New York Review of Books* (April 25, 1985): 34.
33 A. J. Greimas, quoted in Jameson, *Prison-House*, 124.
34 Terence Cave, *The Cornucopian Text: Problems of Writing in the French Renaissance* (Oxford: Oxford University Press, 1974), 100.
35 These are Walser's own words, quoted in Philip Brady, "Little Dancers," *TLS* (December 31, 1993): 17.
36 Roland Barthes, *S/Z* (New York: Hill and Wang, 1974), 132.
37 Pocock, "Texts as Events," 22.
38 See Essay II, pp. 14–15.
39 Robert Frost, quoted in Richard Poirier, *The Performing Self* (New York: Oxford University Press, 1971), 89.
40 P. Klossowski, quoted in Antoine Berman, *The Experience of the Foreign* (Albany: SUNY Press, 1992), 172.
41 *Non intret Cato theatrum meum* ("Let Cato keep out of my theatre"). This sentence is from Martial's own prose preface to Book I of his *Epigrams*, trans. and ed. D. R. Shackleton Bailey (Cambridge, MA: Harvard University Press, 1993), vol. 1, pp. 40–41.
42 Thomas M. Greene, *The Light in Troy* (New Haven: Yale University Press, 1982), 220.
43 Sir Philip Sidney, *Astrophil and Stella*, ed. Max Putzel (Garden City: Doubleday, 1967), 133. The prefatory epistle from which these words are quoted is not by Sidney himself but by Thomas Nashe.
44 Patrick Cheney, "'O, Let My Books Be . . . Dumb Presagers': Poetry and Theater in Shakespeare's Sonnets," *Shakespeare Quarterly* 52, no. 2 (Summer 2001): 241, 224, 243. The quoted passage is from Shakespeare's Sonnet 23 ("As an unperfect actor on the stage"), ll. 9–10.
45 See Essay II, n. 39.
46 Jerzy Kutnik, *The Novel as Performance* (Carbondale: Southern Illinois University Press, 1986).

47 Henry James, *The Scenic Art*, ed. Allan Wade (New York: Hill and Wang, 1957), 3.

48 Jerome McGann, "Marvels and Wonders," *TLS* (December 1, 1995): 6.

49 David Marshall, *The Figure of Theater* (New York: Columbia University Press, 1986), 106.

50 Robert Garis, *The Dickens Theatre* (Oxford: Oxford University Press, 1965), 40.

51 Philip Collins, ed. *Charles Dickens, the Public Readings* (Oxford: Clarendon Press, 1975), xvii.

52 Joseph R. Jones, "Isidore and the Theater," *Comparative Drama* 16, no. 1 (Spring 1982): 32. See, for example, the use of this word in Martial's *Epigrams*, where we read how, in the Roman theatre, a criminal might be put to death by being cast in a scene of evisceration – which was then actually carried out; so that "what had been a play [*fabula*] became an execution." (*De Spectaculis*, Book 9, l. 12, in Martial, *Epigrams*, 18–19).

53 Mary H. Marshall, "*Theatre* in the Middle Ages: Evidence From Dictionaries and Glosses, I," *Speculum* 4, no. 1 (May 1950): 25, 23.

54 William N. West, *Theatres and Encyclopedias in Early Modern Europe* (Cambridge, UK: Cambridge University Press, 2002), 17.

55 Meg Twycross, "Books for the Unlearned," in *Drama and Religion*, ed. James Redmond (Cambridge, UK: Cambridge University Press, 1983), 65. The original Latin text of the quoted phrase is given on p. 107, n. 1.

56 V. A. Kolve, *The Play Called Corpus Christi* (Palo Alto: Stanford University Press, 1966), 5, 25. The phrase "quick book" is from the Lollard antitheatrical *Tretise of Miraclis Pleyinge*. See Woolf, *English Mystery Plays*, 84–86.

57 Michelle P. Brown, *Understanding Illuminated Manuscripts* (Los Angeles: The J. Paul Getty Museum, 1994), 86–87.

58 Pierre Marivaux, *Plays*, ed. Claude Schumacher (London: Methuen, 1988).

59 Henry de Montherlant, *Théâtre* (Paris: Gallimard, 1965).

60 Jerzy Grotowski, *Towards a Poor Theatre* (Holstebro: Odin Teatrets Forlag, 1968), 55–56, 119.

61 Julie Stone Peters, *Theatre of the Book, 1480–1880* (Oxford: Oxford University Press, 2000), 192; and see illus., 107.

62 Ibid.; and note the parallels between Renaissance title pages and allegorical stage tableaux enumerated in Margery Corbett and Ronald Lightman, *The Comely Frontispiece* (London: Routledge & Kegan Paul, 1979), 7.

63 West, *Theatres and Encyclopedias*, 52.

64 Ibid.

65 Sir Philip Sidney, *The Countess of Pembroke's Arcadia (The Old Arcadia)*, ed. Katherine Duncan-Jones (Oxford: Oxford University Press, 1985), 4, 80, 148, 230, 305.

66 A. C. Hamilton, *Sir Philip Sidney* (Cambridge, UK: Cambridge University Press, 1977), 42–43.

67 Sidney, *Arcadia*, ed. Duncan-Jones, x.

68 Ibid., xi.

69 Sir Philip Sidney, *The Countess of Pembroke's Arcadia (The Old Arcadia)*, ed. Jean Robertson (Oxford: The Clarendon Press, 1973), xx; and see Sidney, *Arcadia*, ed. Duncan-Jones, xi n. 13.

70 See Essay II, pp. 18–19, above.

71 Jonas Barish, *The Antitheatrical Prejudice* (Berkeley: University of California Press, 1981), 86, 85.

72   Ibid., 85. On antitheatricalism as itself contributory to theatre, see Martin Puchner, *Stage Fright* (Baltimore: The Johns Hopkins University Press, 2002), 1, 123, 140.

73   Cormac McCarthy, *The Sunset Limited: A Novel in Dramatic Form* (New York: Random House, 2006), 3.

74   Ibid., 114.

75   Ibid., 145.

76   Herman Melville, *Moby-Dick*, ed. Harold Beaver (Harmondsworth: Penguin, 1983). All subsequent chapter and page references to this edition will appear in the text.

77   Other stage directions in what is not yet overtly a script occur on pp. 263 *(Aside)*, 266 *(waving his hand, he moves from the window)* and 267 *(A burst of revelry from the forecastle)*.

78   James Joyce, *Ulysses in Nighttown*, dramatized by Marjorie Barkentin (New York: Random House, 1958). See also Puchner, *Stage Fright*, 97–100.

79   James Joyce, *Ulysses* (New York: Random House, 1934), 431–432. All subsequent page references to this edition will appear in the text. See also Puchner, *Stage Fright*, 80–94.

80   The six cities were: Zurich, London, Paris, New York, Cambridge, Massachusetts and Athens. For the adaptation and production history of *Requiem for a Nun*, see Barbara Izard and Clara Hieronymus, *Requiem for a Nun: Onstage and Off* (Nashville and London: Aurora, 1970), *infra*, and Noel Polk, *Faulkner's Requiem for a Nun: A Critical Study* (Bloomington: Indiana University Press, 1981), 237–245, 268, nn. 1–5.

81   Izard and Hieronymus, *Requiem Onstage*, 181–182, 2.

82   Polk, *Faulkner's Requiem*, 268, n. 5.

83   Izard and Hieronymus, *Requiem Onstage*, 108. See also Polk, *Faulkner's Requiem*, xiv.

84   Polk, *Faulkner's Requiem*, 242. See also Izard and Hieronymus, *Requiem Onstage*, 6.

85   Albert Camus, prefatory note to "*Requiem pour une nonne*," in *l'Avant-scène* no. 407 (July 15, 1968): 8.

86   Polk, *Faulkner's Requiem*, 237; Izard and Hieronymus, *Requiem Onstage*, 1, 3, 14, 162.

87   William Faulkner, *Sanctuary* (New York: New American Library, 1954), chap. 28, pp. 160–164.

88   Ibid., chap. 31, pp. 170–178.

89   Ibid., p. 174.

90   Ibid., chap. 29, p. 164.

91   Ibid., chap. 31, p. 175.

92   Ibid., p. 178.

93   William Faulkner, *Requiem for a Nun* (New York: Random House, 1975), act 2, pp. 110–111.

94   Ibid., p. 117.

95   Ibid., p. 115.

96   Stéphane Mallarmé, "Autobiographie," in *Oeuvres Complètes*, ed. Henri Mondor and G. Jean-Aubry (Paris: Gallimard, 1945), 663.

97   Ibid.

98   These notes were first edited and studied by Jacques Scherer in *Le "Livre" de Mallarmé* (Paris: Gallimard, 1957) and have since been re-edited by Bertrand

Marchal in the new Pléiade edition of Mallarmé's *Oeuvres Complètes* (Paris: Gallimard, 1999). See also Puchner, *Stage Fright*, 67–77.

99 Mallarmé, "Autobiographie," 663.

100 Mary Lewis Shaw teases out a handful of such poetic fragments – see her *Performance in the Texts of Mallarmé* (University Park: Pennsylvania State University Press, 1993), 202–219 – but it takes some teasing.

101 These specifics have been culled from Shaw, *Performance*, 187–188 and from Richard Sieburth, "The Master's Testament," *TLS* (October 15, 1999): 4.

102 Sieburth, "Master's Testament," 4.

103 Scherer, *Le "Livre"*, 35.

104 Shaw, *Performance*, 200.

105 Sieburth, "Master's Testament," 4.

106 Leo Bersani, *The Death of Stéphane Mallarmé* (Cambridge, UK: Cambridge University Press, 1982), 55.

107 Sieburth, "Master's Testament," 4. The word "événement" is Sieburth's. not Mallarmé's.

108 See Essay II, pp. 14–16, above.

109 See Essay II, p. 16, above.

110 See Essay II, pp. 16–18, above.

111 See Hans-Thies Lehmann, *Postdramatic Theatre*, trans. Karen Jürs-Murphy (London and New York: Routledge, 2006), 6, 9, 17, 85–86 and Richard Schechner, *Performance Studies: An Introduction*, 2nd edition (New York and London: Routledge, 2006), 227.

Essay III The theatre wants
to go in

There is a comparison heard all the time in our cultural discourse, yet apparently so off the mark that the wonder is it should ever have been made at all:

> The aim of the lyric poem is to show what is going on in the theater of
> the private mind.[1]
> [C]oncepts behave much as percepts do in the theater of mind.[2]
> These psychic plays may be performed in the theater of our own minds.[3]
> Why, in the theater of the mind, are you You? *You* and not *me*?[4]
> . . . the theatre of the mind alone.[5]

Theatre is the most public of arts, transacted among persons, before persons, in some shared civic space (market square, cathedral porch, opera house). As such, it might appear a most unlikely source of images for inner experience; and yet it cannot seem to stop supplying them. Our minds, we are assured, are *inner theatres* ("It is the inner theatre that is costumed by the choice in clothes"),[6] in which, after *inner rehearsal*,[7] an *inner drama*[8] is mounted on an *inner stage* ("*scène intérieure*").[9] Before this *mental performance*,[10] "my Mind sits as a Spectator"[11] – a *mental spectator*[12] in a *mental theatre*,[13] where "some of my Thoughts make Plays, and others Act those Plays."[14]

Consciousness is "the stage for it all to happen [on],"[15] except, of course, for what happens on "the busy lit stage of [the] subconscious."[16] One's heart may be "nothing but a stage for tragedies";[17] one's imagination is "capable of having . . . scenes acted upon it."[18] Memories, claims Freud, "are analogous to theatrical performances [*Darstellungen auf der Bühne*]";[19] a dream, according to Jung, is "a theater"[20] – necessarily, a "private theater,"[21] a "secret theater,"[22] a "theater of soul."[23]

This strain of imagery is especially popular with writers and critics of literature. Victor Hugo, for example, referred to "that ideal theatre which every man has in his mind";[24] while his Old Historicist contemporary,

Hyppolite Taine, proposed to "compare the mind of man to a theater."[25] But one also comes on inner theatres in the writings of psychologists, art critics, neuroscientists, theologians. . . .

The appeal of this image to author after author in field after field is not far to seek. It fulfills, in equal measure, two powerful and, one might have thought, irreconcilable fantasies. On the one hand, when Freud's patient Anna O. describes the systematic day-dreaming by which she enlivens a drab existence as her "private theatre,"[26] she is clearly exerting an introjective will-to-power over an otherwise intractable external reality. Traditionally, theatre takes in the world; let me have "taken in" the theatre, and the world is mine. And, having once become, in Robert Burton's phrase, "a theatre to myself,"[27] what prevents my henceforth assuming every role in the house? "The dreamer is scene, player, prompter, director, author, audience, and critic";[28] he "preside[s] above the busy lit stage of his subconscious as prompter and playwright, audience and deus ex machina as well as hero."[29]

But if the inner theatre metaphor feeds fantasies of impregnable self-containment, it may as readily give expression to a quite contrary hope. In *The Interpretation of Dreams*, Freud characterizes our unconscious life as "an other scene [*eine andere Schauplatz*]."[30] A *Schauplatz* is a public theatre or other viewing place. If my unconscious life goes forward on a *Schauplatz*, it is no less available to be witnessed and shared (at least by the trained analyst/spectator) than is a theatre performance. My "inner" or "secret" or "private" theatre has become a show in a showplace.

It is not, however, the use made of inner theatre imagery by writers in other fields that chiefly interests me. Here is an image that seems to know something *about theatre* that theatre doesn't know about itself. What if we were to turn it back on theatre and let it tell what it knows.

I will anticipate the outcome of such a reversal so far as this: The pervasive use of theatre as a trope for all sorts of inward processes, faculties and activities, if it goes against the overt nature of theatre as public, interpersonal event, also picks up something essential about it, namely, that in some sense or senses, *the theatre wants to go in*.

It is not difficult to produce evidence for this proposition; the difficulty lies in coming to see it all as evidence for a single proposition. No very exotic items appear on the following list:

- backstage
- offstage
- inner stage[31]
- dressing room[32]
- green room
- subtext

- inner life of character
- working from the outside in
- closed rehearsal
- play within a play
- closet drama

Whether considered as a physical place (with its back-, off-, and inner stage, its green room and dressing rooms), as a set of practices (the search for subtexts and inner life, "working from the outside in," closed rehearsals), as a corpus of texts (some "within" others, some meant for solitary reading), plainly theatre looks within, turns in upon itself, draws inward, has an affinity for the inside, *has* an inside – in short, is no stranger to that inwardness which the long line of inner/mental/private theatre images we started with may have seemed, against theatre's nature, to be foisting upon it.

How is any such inwardness related to the far more evident character of theatre as a shared, witnessed event transacted among persons in a public space?

We might look first at the structure of theatre buildings as both figuring and instancing this relationship. Pretty much any theatre is going to consist of an *outward*-looking space (a stage or other playing area – an *on*stage) and a network of *inner* spaces (prop room, costume cage, green room, dressing rooms, offices – an *off*stage). Stated thus, the contrast a theatre building seems to offer between outer and inner theatre sounds pretty absolute. Yet between this outer and this inner there are continuities. The stage visibly contains, and frankly displays, pockets of offstage. Teasers and tormentors force the presence of a concealed "within" upon the notice of those (the audience) from whom they conceal it. Flies overhead and traps in the stage floor betray the near-adjacency of an upper and lower "within."

And, of course, between this without and this within, *there is passage*, which is to say, there are passages. Outer and inner theatre, offstage and on, are linked, in a proscenium theatre by wings, in the Greek theatre by *parodoi* (side-ramps), in a modern thrust-stage theatre by some system of ramps and aisles descended from the Greek *parodos*, and in a present-day immersive or site-specific performance space by their having been the same place to begin with.

Along such passageways, only movement in one direction tends to interest us: from rehearsal hall to performance space, from green room to stage (and, one must add, from text to event; for, as I showed in Essay II, it is the claim of *every* text to be, in the end, an event, that a staged *dramatic* text enacts on behalf of them all). Here, we tend to feel, is the true theatrical trajectory.

The reverse transit – from onstage to off, from without to within, from event to text – only occurs when, and can only mean that, the show is over.

But are these "opposed" directions really all that implacably opposed? Can they, even, always be very clearly distinguished? In Baroque perspectival settings, the vanishing point was often located some ways upstage of the most upstage-center flat or drop.[33] Were audiences meant to view a vanishing point thus placed as farthest *out* or deepest *in*? In the Elizabethan playhouse "[a] character leaving the stage goes 'within' from the point of view of the actors and goes 'out' from that of the spectators."[34] How distinct was this *out* from this *within*? Not very, according to the Clown in one Elizabethan play, who, responding to the summons "Within there!," enters proclaiming: "Within there is now without here!"[35]

Anticipating as it does by several centuries Tom Stoppard's epigram that "every exit [is] an entrance somewhere else,"[36] this quibble suggests that Stoppard's Player should be heard as delivering not a deep metaphysical paradox about *inner* vs. *outer* but merely a plain truth about theatre. Or maybe plain truths about theatre cannot help but acquire the status of deep metaphysical paradoxes. Nothing, I suspect, was farther from Dickens' mind than metaphysics when he described Little Dorrit's visit backstage to see her dancer-sister as follows:

> At last they came into a maze of dust, where a quantity of people were tumbling over one another, and where there was such a confusion of unaccountable shapes of beams, bulkheads, brick walls, ropes, and rollers, and such a mixing of gaslight and daylight that they seemed to have got on the wrong side of the pattern of the universe.[37]

And yet, Dorrit's transit suggests nothing so much as the paradoxical itinerary of her visionary contemporary, Emily Dickinson, who likewise could manage small certainty as to whether hers had been a journey out or journey in:

> I saw no way – The heavens were stitched –
> I felt the Columns close –
> The Earth reversed her Hemispheres –
> I touched the Universe –
>
> And back it slid –[38]

What if, encouraged by such ambiguities as these in the physical layout of theatres, we resolved to find theatre no less in its moment of indrawing than outpouring – what should we find? To what condition or state does theatre, in thus "going in," withdraw – and where, if we were to go in after it, should we find ourselves?

Most of the "inner theatre" references one comes upon are too fleeting to be of much help in answering these questions. When Luce Irigaray characterizes the (male) soul as "that theater for the re-presentation of likeness"[39] or Emily Dickinson describes "the Human Heart" as "Only Theatre recorded/Owner cannot shut,"[40] these are certainly suggestive formulations, but how shall we advance beyond suggestion? Exactly what, and exactly where, is this "within" toward which *off*stage and *closed* rehearsals and *sub*texts and *closet* dramas all seem to gesture?

I will now examine two portrayals of inner theatres sufficiently sustained to allow speculation on this point. The devisers of these two "theatres" could not be more unlike: one, Giulio Camillo, was a sixteenth-century practitioner of Hermetic-Cabalistic magic; the other, David Hume, was an eighteenth-century rationalist philosopher. It is all the more striking – and a big hint of what is at stake in this symbolism – that inner theatres should figure in the thought of both.

The so-called "Memory Theatre" of Giulio Camillo, as sketched out in his *L'Idea del Theatro* (1550), was apparently intended as the blueprint for an actual theatre.[41] The design was never realized, the theatre never built (though a largescale wooden maquette seems to have been). But whether in space or only on paper, what Camillo sought to represent was the mind in recollection as a kind of theatre building.

As Frances Yates has shown, since antiquity there had existed a technique for memorizing long lists of words or ideas by mentally "placing" each item at some point in a familiar room or scene and then moving in thought from point to point, retrieving, at each, the item placed there. Over the centuries, all manner of sites had been thus pressed into service as memory "places." The words or names or thoughts to be recalled might be placed along the successive courtyards of a palace, sections of a cathedral, or spheres of the Ptolemaic universe. Camillo, however, was the first to propose placing them around a *theatre*, specifically, a Greco-Roman theatre of Vitruvian design, consisting of seven semi-circular rows of seats rising each above last in concentric tiers and sliced into like a pie by seven radial aisles or gangways, thus creating 49 (7×7) memory places.

For the retrieval of what material was this vast *aide-mémoire* intended? Frances Yates herself, believing that by the Renaissance "[t]he art of memory has become an occult art,"[42] argues that Camillo's "Theatre is . . . a vision of the world and of the nature of things, seen from a height, from the stars,"[43] so that "if we go up the Theatre, by the gangways of the seven planets, the whole creation falls into order."[44] Perhaps; but according to a contemporary who had actually examined Camillo's maquette, the theatre's

49 memory places were in fact "drawers, or boxes, or coffers of some kind containing masses of papers, and on these papers were speeches based on the works of Cicero."[45] This account suggests that Camillo's *theatro* was less a model of the cosmos than "a method of arranging and storing passages from Cicero by topic," a sort of 49-volume encyclopedia.[46]

Whatever the exact nature of the texts deployed in what Yates herself calls "a highly ornamental filing cabinet,"[47] an array of *texts* it most surely was. For note: there is *no stage* in Camillo's memory theatre: where stage and actors would normally stand in a Vitruvian theatre, there stands only the would-be rememberer/reader. And there is *no audience*: what would normally be the seating area of a Vitruvian theatre is occupied by that 7 × 7 "filing cabinet" of Ciceronian fragments. This "theatre" is *all text*, which amounts to saying that, in the present instance at least, what an "inner theatre" turns out to be is a text. Let us consider another instance.

Even for a mental construct, David Hume's inner theatre is a strangely phantasmal place:

> The mind is a kind of theatre, where several perceptions successively make their appearance; pass, re-pass, glide away, and mingle in an infinite variety of postures and situations.[48]

And no sooner has Hume ventured his mind–theatre comparison than he appears to snatch it back or at least severely qualify it:

> The comparison of the theatre must not mislead us. They are the successive perceptions only, that constitute the mind; nor have we the most distant notion of the place, where these scenes are represented, or of the materials, of which it is compos'd.[49]

In fact, this anxious retraction of the theatre-image suggests the motive for its initial adoption.

For of course one has been in this "theatre" before, any time one has dipped into a poststructuralist account of writers and writing. For the poststructuralists, too, "it is a matter of depriving the subject . . . of its role as originator";[50] the author, they hold, "is born simultaneously with the text, is in no way equipped with a being preceding or exceeding the writing."[51] Like Hume's mind, where perceptions "pass, re-pass, glide away," Roland Barthes' text "is . . . passage, traversal."[52] And like Hume's theatre of mind, Barthes' text "is experienced only in an activity, a production,"[53] a production where "only language acts, 'performs,' and not 'me'."[54] In each case we must avoid the same "error": that of postulating some prior self before which passes (Hume) that "infinite variety of postures and situations" – there is only the infinite variety – or from which issues (Barthes, Foucault) the ceaseless flow of words – there is only the ceaseless flow.[55]

In short, no less than Camillo's memory theatre, Hume's theatre of mind gives every indication of being a text. Of course, Camillo's and Hume's conceptions of a text are very different. For Camillo, the Renaissance sage, a text is a fixed, ordered arrangement of classical borrowings (that 7×7 "filing cabinet" of excerpts from Cicero). For Hume, the (post?)modern skeptic, a text is a "glid[ing]" succession of (dis)appearances. What does it say *about theatre* that "inner theatre" can equally well stand for the text on two such unlike views of the text? Surely the implication is that, however conceived, a text is theatre that has "gone in," that what theatre "goes in" to be is a text.

This is not to say that any time there is talk of inner (or private or mental) theatres, we are hearing about texts. On occasion, this comes near being the case. The "theatre" to which Jung, and the "other scene" to which Freud, liken inner experience are clearly texts in want of reading.[56] But other times (as with Valéry's "Why, in the theater of the mind, are you *You . . .* and not *me*?"),[57] we lack sufficient information to say whether an *inner theatre/text* equivalence is being asserted; and clearly sometimes (as with Anne Hollander's "inner theatre . . . costumed by the choice in clothes"),[58] none is.

But all this is scarcely our concern. We are not, recall, reading the "inner theatre" image for what it tells us about the various disciplines or situations to which it may be applied but for what its being thus applicable tells us *about theatre*. And what it tells us is that the "within" to which, in case after case, theatre withdraws, is a text.

That text may be a *poem*:

> [Mallarmé] had initially conceived his two great poems [*Hérodiade* and *l'Après-midi d'un Faune*] for the stage. . . . But the longer he worked on them, the more distinctly they tended to evolve from actual to mental theatre [*théâtre de l'esprit*].[59]

or a *novel*:

> The process that had begun with the move into an indoor, darkened theater reached its climax in the novel, that private theater in the innermost darkness of the individual mind.[60]

or simply a *book*:

> And isn't the book the internalization of theater, the inner stage?[61]

Most often, though, the text into which theatre withdraws is a *dramatic* text. "The script," as one critic puts it, "stores the play."[62] But the relation is a more dynamic one than mere storage. As I observed in *Acting as Reading*:

> We are accustomed to speak of the action of a play as being intermittently "realized" in performance. But couldn't one as well say (in fact, wouldn't it be *truer to experience* to say) that, between occasions when it is performed, the action of a play is intermittently "derealized" in its script, that the script is where the events of the play "go" when they cannot be an event just then? Certainly, this is how dramatic texts present themselves – that is, as events that have unaccountably "lapsed" from their event-status into mere writing and are going to have to be "rescued" from this (no doubt temporary) humiliation.[63]

This perspective finds expression in the common French practice, noted in Essay II, of titling a volume of plays by a single playwright the "Theatre" of that playwright. Between productions, the theatre of Montherlant goes in to be the *Théâtre de Montherlant*.

There is no era of Western drama that does not afford instances of the dramatic text regarded as theatre "gone in." Attic tragedy may originally have been intended for performance but "[by] the end of the fifth century, the Greek plays were circulated as books and so became a kind of *Lesedrama* [theatre for reading]."[64] The texts of the medieval liturgical and cycle plays were transcribed into books of every description (breviaries, antiphonars, tropers, Bible manuscripts),[65] their very moments of stage business "passing inward" to become illustrations of volumes like *The Holkham Bible Picture Book*.[66] Just such a stage-to-page trajectory seems reflected in the evolution of the medieval Latin theatrical term *scaena*, which went from meaning a small, sheltered *playing area* to denoting, like its modern English cognate, a segment of the *script* ("Act II, scene i").[67] And when, in the mid-seventeenth century, religion, which had once fostered the theatres of England, shuttered them, "[t]he paradoxical result was that many plays were transcribed and circulated in print that would otherwise have been lost."[68]

The nineteenth century is often regarded, at least in Britain, as an era of theatrical downturn. But there is some evidence that the dramatic monologue, that "merely literary" genre generally supposed to have flourished in the absence of, and at the expense of, theatre, may better be understood as a form of theatre "gone in." Tennyson, a chief practitioner of the genre, described his dramatic monologue *Maud* as "a drama where successive phases of passion in one person take the place of successive persons."[69] This may seem no more than a convenient distinction. But, as Dwight Culler has shown, there existed in the late eighteenth and early nineteenth centuries an actual mode of theatre performance – Rousseau and Goethe were among those supplying texts for it[70] – where a single actor did in fact come before an audience and present "successive phases of passion in one person." Emma Hamilton, in whose one-woman shows Goethe observed how "sad, playful, exultant, repentant, wanton, menacing, anxious – all mental states follow rapidly one after another,"[71] was a noted performer of these so-called monodramas. Shall we not see, in dramatic monologues like "Abt Vogler" and "Fra Lippo Lippi," instances of just such "monodramatic" theatre performances that have "gone in" to become texts?

Another indication of theatre's nineteenth-century turn inward is the Romantic exaltation of private, silent playreading over stage productions. Such a preference, of course, long predates the Romantics – Horace, Jonson and Dryden had all advocated for what Richard Flecknoe, in his *Short Discourse of the English Stage* (1664), memorably called "the solid joy of the interior"[72] – and continued to find champions long after them: Conrad, Anatole France and (the playwright!) Maeterlinck each held some version of Karl Kraus's view that "[t]he dramatic work of art has no business on the stage."[73]

Still, the Romantic era is the great age of silent, solitary playreading, not so much because there was now more of it as because larger and different claims were now being made for it. As one would expect, such claims often came at the expense of theatre and theatregoing. If "[w]e do not like to see our author's plays acted, and least of all, *Hamlet*,"[74] if "the Lear of Shakespeare cannot be acted,"[75] if, in general, "the plays of Shakespeare are less calculated for performance . . . than those of almost any other dramatist,"[76] this can only mean that "[p]oetry and the stage do not agree well together."[77]

Since it was the early nineteenth-century London stage from which Hazlitt, Coleridge and Lamb thus ran screaming, one is tempted to attribute their flight to the vulgarity of contemporary productions; but in truth *production* is the vulgarity. On any stage, "[t]hat which was [in the text] merely an airy shape, a dream, a passing thought, immediately becomes an unmanageable reality."[78] Shakespeare, and arguably every true dramatist, must "find his proper place in the heart and in the closet."[79] All theatre aspires to the condition of closet drama (in which, not coincidentally, the nineteenth century abounded), that is, to the condition of a text read silently to oneself in a room.

This looks like a straightforward cherishing of the literary over the theatrical. But we must not miss the paradox. Clearly, the proper place for drama is the theatre. If drama's proper place is henceforth to be the closet of solitary reading, this can only mean that the solitary reader's closet must henceforth be recognized as the true theatre, i.e., that theatre has "gone in" to be the reading of a text.

Something like this trajectory seems forecast in that granddaddy of all closet dramas, the "closet scene" (III.iv) from *Hamlet*.[80] It may appear perverse to seek a prototype of the unstaged in this most staged of plays. But this is the very anomaly that the closet scene itself sets out to explore.

Hamlet famously likens acting to "a mirror [held] up to nature,"[81] a figure that lays stress on theatre's out-and-about, world-surveying character. Yet when Hamlet himself now comes to hold up a (metaphorical) mirror – "You go not till I set you up a glass/Where you may see the inmost part of you"[82] – it is to one person, his mother, alone in her closet.[83] This may seem a strangely inward turn for the image of theatre as nature's mirror to have taken, until we set beside it the advice a contemporary of Shakespeare's offered his female readers: "Make then your Chamber your private Theatre."[84] True, unlike Hazlitt and Lamb, Gertrude before the "glass" in her private closet/theatre does no actual reading. But, as the titles of numberless medieval and Renaissance works suggest – *Speculum humanae salvationis*, *A Mirror for Magistrates*, etc. – there is a long tradition of equating mirrors and books.[85] And in fact the "black and grainèd spots" that Gertrude tells Hamlet she sees when "[t]hou turn'st mine eyes into my very soul" sound like nothing so much as print forced upon the attention of a (reluctant) reader.[86]

Still, outside of Gertrude's closet, the distinction between performing a text and merely reading it seems plain enough, and to declare the mere reading the true performance has the ring of an antitheatricalist paradox. I would, however, note the presence of something like this perspective in the work of a critic to whom no taint of antitheatricalism attaches. In *The Actor's Freedom* Michael Goldman maintains that the heroes of comedies "exhibit an appealing freedom, clearly associated with the actor's";[87] likewise, the hero of a script by Brecht or Pirandello "can be perceived almost transparently as an actor."[88] Nor is it only comic and theatricalist protagonists who ask to be seen this way; in every script "the hero . . . is always in some sense an actor who carries his acting to an extreme."[89] And not just the hero: "In any good play, the principal characters go beyond ordinary bounds in ways that remind us of acting."[90] Across the board, "[t]he characters of drama are actors."[91] We may wish to press the distinction between *reading a text* and *giving a performance*. But, Goldman implies, on first taking up the script we shall find the performance we seek to distinguish it from already in progress. For what is performance but "a matter of . . . showing how the character *acts*"?[92] – and who more clearly shows this than the character him or herself?

***

To propose Solomon's Temple in Jerusalem as some sort of prototype for theatre may seem preposterous. To propose the relation between the Temple's inmost recess, the Holy of Holies, and later Jewish textual tradition as the prototype for theatre's passing inward may seem only slightly less so. If, nevertheless, I do now pursue these connections, it is not so much a further step in the argument I have been making as an image of that argument overall.

Despite the obvious tension between Jewish Temple worship and dramatic performance – the Second Commandment forbids representation, the rabbis disparaged theatregoing,[93] etc. – I am far from the first to have sensed a link between them. Inigo Jones offered an account of Stonehenge as "an ancient Roman theatre-temple [that] easily transposes into the Temple at Jerusalem."[94] Philip II based the design of his Escorial palace "on the plan of the ancient theatre combined with that of the Temple of Solomon."[95]

Unlikely as any such temple/theatre conjunction may sound, it rests upon a whole series of specific parallels. At both Jerusalem and Athens, participants in a multi-day festival (Passover, the City Dionysia) "went up" to a cultic center (the Temple, the Theatre of Dionysus) in their respective cultural capitals to worship an exigent god (Yahweh, Bacchus). Both festivals featured processions, sacrifices and choral singing (the Psalms, dithyramb).[96]

To this whole line of comparison, however, there would seem to be one fatal objection. On the dancing-floor of the Theatre of Dionysus in Athens there appeared, at length, actors performing actions. In the Holy of Holies of the Jerusalem Temple, there appeared – nothing. When, once a year, on the Day of Atonement, the High Priest entered the inmost sanctum,[97] he found himself in a (nearly) empty room. Of course, near-emptiness scarcely disqualifies a place to be a point of theatrical origins. Indeed, the traditional site of Western theatre's beginnings – the tomb from which, in the course of the *quem quaeritis*-exchange, Christ is found to have decamped – is just such another come-upon emptiness.[98] *Non est hic*. . . . What is any theatre but an initially "empty space" . . . which now begins to fill?

Only two objects are known for certain to have been present in the Holy of Holies when the High Priest annually breached it – and both have overtones of theatre. These were:

1   a veil that set the place off from the rest of the Temple and the world,[99] i.e., a "curtain"
2   the original Tablets of the Law handed down to Moses on Sinai,[100] i.e., a text enjoining certain actions, a "script"[101]

When now the veil/"curtain" "rose" and the priestly "performer" confronted the Tablets/"script," this all-but-empty space did indeed begin to fill . . . with persons, voices, images, events. For, rabbinic tradition assures us, the High Priest, as he moved through the Holy of Holies, crossed paths with spectral others,[102] heard heavenly voices,[103] beheld God seated on His throne and engaged in dialogue with Him:

> Rabbi Ishmael ben Elisha said, "Once when I entered the Holy of Holies . . . I saw the crowned God, the Lord of Hosts, seated on a lofty and exalted throne. He said to me, 'Ishmael, My son, bless Me.' I said to Him, 'May it be Your will that Your mercy overcome Your anger. . . .' He nodded His head in assent."[104]

In 70 AD the Roman Emperor Titus laid siege to Jerusalem and demolished the Temple; in the rubble of the Holy of Holies, foxes now roamed.[105] Whatever interest may be possessed by the Temple/theatre analogy I have been pressing, here might seem to be the end of it. But in fact, it is only now that the full force and true interest of the parallel for our inquiry first appears.

"From the day that the Holy Temple was destroyed, the Holy One, blessed be He, dwelt only within the structure of the *halakha*," declared an early rabbi, Hiya bar Ami.[106] *Halakha* is the Jewish written law as preserved in the Talmud, i.e., in a book. *A book* thus replaces the Temple as "the lone remaining structure of Judaism,"[107] which is to say, as the lone remaining site of theatre. While the Temple stood, a celebrant ventured within the theatrelike Holy of Holies to perform his encounter with the divine. Now, with the Temple gone, a Holy Book takes the place of the Holy of Holies, and what is performed is an interpretation of that book, is reading.

Where theatre was, text shall be – here is the trajectory we have already traced for closet drama, for the dramatic monologue, for Camillo's memory theatre. . . . That it should turn out to be, as well, the trajectory of Jewish textual tradition – from Holy of Holies to Holy Book – is what qualifies the Jerusalem Temple, "gone in" to be the Talmud, to stand as our image of inner theatre.

As no more than an image, to be sure. And in truth this whole vocabulary of "inner theatre," "theatre 'going in'" may be no more than a manner of speaking. It is, however, a manner of speaking confidently. We worry the distinction – and worry ourselves over the distinction – between the literary and the theatrical, text and performance, page and stage. Theatre, however, knows better, and shows its better knowledge in recognizing the literary as, merely, the theatrical fled back up the *parodos* to be, for a time, literature – the countermove to that "breaking forth as event," traced in Essay II, whereby staged dramatic texts enact the claim of texts one and all to be, after all, events.

Where theatre was, text shall be – a text, however, that represents not an alternative to theatre but the site of theatre's own going in to be that very text.

Notes

1 Helen Vendler, "A New Way of Being," *Radcliffe Quarterly* 85, no. 3 (Winter 2000): 6.
2 Bernard J. Baars, *In the Theater of Consciousness* (New York: Oxford University Press, 1997), 87.
3 Joyce McDougall, *Theaters of the Mind: Illusion and Truth on the Psychoanalytic Stage* (New York: Brunner/Mazel, 1991), 4.
4 Paul Valéry, *Monsieur Teste* (Princeton: Princeton University Press, 1973), 70.
5 Stéphane Mallarmé, quoted in Janet Ruth Heller, *Coleridge, Lamb, Hazlitt and the Reader of Drama* (Columbia: University of Missouri Press, 1990), 131.
6 Anne Hollander, *Seeing Through Clothes* (New York: Avon, 1980), 451.
7 Baars, *In the Theater of Consciousness*, 7.
8 Vendler, "A New Way of Being," 6.
9 Stéphane Mallarmé, quoted in Eric Benoit, *Mallarmé et le mystère du "Livre"* (Paris: Honoré Champion, 1998), 59.
10 Thomas Hardy, *The Dynasts* (London: Macmillan, 1965), Preface, xxvi.
11 Margaret Cavendish, quoted in Marta Straznicky, *Privacy, Playreading, and Women's Closet Drama, 1550–1700* (Cambridge, UK: Cambridge University Press, 2004), 84.
12 Hardy, *The Dynasts*, Preface, xxv.
13 Lord Byron, August 23, 1821 letter, quoted in Patricia Ball, *The Central Self: A Study in Romantic and Victorian Imagination* (London: Athalone, 1968), 41.
14 Margaret Cavendish, quoted in Straznicky, *Privacy, Playreading and Women's Closet Drama*, 83–84.
15 John J. Ratey, *A User's Guide to the Brain: Perception, Attention, and the Four Theaters of the Brain* (New York: Pantheon, 2001), 341.
16 John Updike, "Short Easter," *The New Yorker* (March 27, 1989): 42.
17 Sir Philip Sidney, *The Countess of Pembroke's Arcadia (The New Arcadia)*, ed. Maurice Evans (Harmondsworth: Penguin, 1987), 126.
18 Sixteenth-century theologian Thomas Burnet, quoted in William Kerrigan, *The Prophetic Milton* (Charlottesville: University of Virginia Press, 1974), 112.
19 Sigmund Freud, quoted in Sarah Kofman, *The Childhood of Art* (New York: Columbia University Press, 1988), 60.
20 Carl Jung, quoted in Ken Frieden, *Freud's Dream of Interpretation* (Albany: SUNY Press, 1990), 4.
21 Quentin Anderson, *The Imperial Self* (New York: Knopf, 1971), 41.
22 McDougall, *Theaters of the Mind*, 286.
23 Anderson, *Imperial Self*, 104.
24 Victor Hugo, quoted in Evlyn Gould, *Virtual Theater From Diderot to Mallarmé* (Baltimore: Johns Hopkins University Press, 1989), 78 (my translation).
25 Hyppolite Taine, quoted in Baars, *In the Theater of Consciousness*, 52.
26 Sigmund Freud and Josef Breuer, *Studies on Hysteria* (Harmondsworth: Penguin, 1974), 74.
27 Robert Burton, *The Anatomy of Melancholy*, ed. Floyd Dell and Paul Jordan-Smith (New York: Tudor, 1955), 14.

28 Carl Jung, quoted in Frieden, *Freud's Dream of Interpretation*, 4.

29 Updike, "Short Easter," 42.

30 Sigmund Freud, *The Interpretation of Dreams* (New York: Avon, 1971), 81, 574. See also J. Laplanche and J.-B. Pontalis, *The Language of Psychoanalysis* (New York: Norton, 1973), 450.

31 There is, of course, a longrunning scholarly debate as to whether any such structure as an "inner stage" ever made part of Elizabethan playhouses. Older theatre historians felt no uncertainty on this score. For George Kernodle, the inner stage was London's version of the Italian *nicho*, an upstage-center playing area in use, "principally for interior scenes . . . all over Europe" (George R. Kernodle, *From Art to Theatre* [Chicago: The University of Chicago Press, 1944], 157). Ashley Thorndike viewed the Elizabethan inner stage, "expanded in depth and size," as the prototype of "the picture-frame stage of today" (Ashley H. Thorndike, *Shakespeare's Theater* [New York: Macmillan, 1960], 77). But as long ago as 1961 Richard Southern expressed doubts as to the very existence of inner stages: "there is," he pointed out, "no use of the term 'inner stage' in all of Elizabethan literature" (Richard Southern, *The Seven Ages of the Theatre* [New York: Hill and Wang, 1961], 183). I have no competence to participate in this debate. I would only observe that among the sorts of places that inner stages, if such there ever were, are thought to have represented were bedrooms and studies (Thorndike, *Shakespeare's Theater*, 74) – likely sites, both, for at least one of the modes of "inner theatre" we shall presently consider: solitary playreading – and, surprisingly, shops (ibid., 85–86, 127). Or maybe not so surprisingly. Already in Shakespeare's time Montaigne's "back shop all our own" (*arrière-boutique toute nôtre*), "in which to establish our principal retreat and solitude," was a familiar image of interior life. (See Michel de Montaigne, "Of Solitude," in *Essays and Selected Writings*, trans. Donald M. Frame [New York: St Martins, 1963], 122–123).

32 Dressing rooms in the Elizabethan theatre were called "tiring houses"; see, for example, Ben Jonson, *Poetaster*, ed. Tom Cain (Manchester: Manchester University Press, 1995), V.iii.577–78n, p. 257. It is tempting, for one in search of theatrical inner spaces, to take the first word of this phrase as short for "retiring" (even as the first word of "drawing room" is short for "withdrawing"). Tempting, but wrong: A tiring house was so named because it was where actors went to change into and out of their "tires" – "dress, apparel, raiment" (*OED*, "tire," 2) – as in Cleopatra's reference to having dressed Antony in "my tires" (William Shakespeare, *Antony and Cleopatra*, ed. Barbara Everett [New York: Signet, 1998], II.v.22, p. 44); compare the modern English word "attire." Nevertheless, a text of 1610 refers to a bishop's country retreat as his "retiring House" (*OED*, "retiring," 2.*attrib*.a); and it is no great stretch to see Elizabethan actors' tiring houses as having been what dressing rooms have always been for actors: places of mental retirement/withdrawal deep within theatres.

33 Kernodle, *From Art to Theatre*, 179.

34 W. W. Greg, *Dramatic Documents From the Elizabethan Playhouses: Commentary* (Oxford: Oxford University Press, 1969), 208.

35 Quoted in Greg, *Dramatic Documents*, 209.

36 Tom Stoppard, *Rosencrantz and Guildenstern Are Dead* (New York: Grove Press, 1967), Act I, p. 28.

37 Charles Dickens, *Little Dorrit* (New York: The Heritage Press, 1956), chap. 20, p. 228.

38 Emily Dickinson, *Complete Poems*, ed. Thomas H. Johnson (Boston: Little, Brown, 1960), Poem #378 ("I saw no way"), ll. 1–5, p. 180.

39 Luce Irigaray, *Speculum of the Other Woman* (Ithaca: Cornell University Press, 1985), 362.

40 Dickinson, *Complete Poems*, Poem #741 ("Drama's Vitallest Expression"), ll. 14–15, p. 363.

41 For Camillo and the mnemonic tradition in which he worked, see Frances A. Yates, *The Art of Memory* (Harmondsworth: Penguin, 1969), especially chap. 6, pp. 135–174, on which the following discussion is largely based.

42 Ibid., 161.

43 Ibid., 148.

44 Ibid., 146.

45 Ibid., 148.

46 William N. West, *Theatres and Encyclopedias in Early Modern Europe* (Cambridge, UK: Cambridge University Press, 2002), 85.

47 Yates, *Art of Memory*, 149.

48 David Hume, *A Treatise of Human Nature* (London: Penguin, 1987), Book 1, Part 4, Section 6, p. 301.

49 Ibid.

50 Michel Foucault, "What Is an Author?" in *Textual Strategies*, ed. Josué V. Harari (Ithaca: Cornell University Press, 1979), 158.

51 Roland Barthes, "The Death of the Author," in *Image-Music-Text* (New York: Hill and Wang, 1982), 145.

52 Roland Barthes, "From Work to Text," in Harari, *Textual Strategies*, 76.

53 Ibid., 75.

54 Barthes, "Death of the Author," 143.

55 Hume's equating of the textlike human mind to an inner theatre receives considerable support from his attributing to the workings of that mind the "infinite variety" of Shakespeare's most theatrical character. (See Shakespeare, *Antony and Cleopatra*, II.ii.242, p. 39.) It is as if, deep within our minds, something like a performance of *Antony and Cleopatra* were always in progress, our minds, indeed, being best understood as the progress of just such a performance.

56 See above, Essay III, nn. 19–20 and n. 30.

57 See above, Essay III, n. 4.

58 See above, Essay III, n. 6.

59 Jacques Scherer, *Le "Livre" de Mallarmé* (Paris: Gallimard, 1957), 10 (my translation).

60 Leslie A. Fiedler, *Love and Death in the American Novel* (New York: Stein and Day, 1975), 44. In *Empty Houses: Theatrical Failure and the Novel* (Princeton: Princeton University Press, 2012), David Kurnick explores the consequences for modern fiction of "the 'novelization' (that is, the interiorization) of the theater" (194) in the thinking and practice of certain nineteenth- and twentieth-century novelists.

61 Jacques Derrida, *Dissemination* (Chicago: University of Chicago Press, 1981), 233.

62 Stanley Everden, quoted in Shou-ren Wang, *The Theatre of the Mind* (London: Macmillan, 1989), xi.

63 David Cole, *Acting as Reading* (Ann Arbor: University of Michigan Press, 1992), 136.
64 Norman T. Pratt, *Seneca's Drama* (Chapel Hill: University of North Carolina Press, 1983), 20.
65 Rosemary Woolf, *The English Mystery Plays* (Berkeley: University of California Press, 1972), 21, 153, 43.
66 V. A. Kolve, *The Play Called Corpus Christi* (Stanford: Stanford University Press, 1966), 38.
67 Mary H. Marshall, "*Theatre* in the Middle Ages: Evidence From Dictionaries and Glosses, I," *Symposium* 4, no. 1 (May 1950): 24–25. See my account of these dual senses of *scaena* in Essay II, pp. 18–19.
68 Andrew Hadfield, "Editor as Censor," *TLS* (February 20, 2004): 26.
69 Alfred Lord Tennyson, quoted in A. Dwight Culler, "Monodrama and the Dramatic Monologue," *PMLA* 90, no. 2 (April 1975): 369.
70 Culler, "Monodrama and the Dramatic Monologue," 370–371.
71 Johann Wolfgang von Goethe, quoted in Culler, "Monodrama and the Dramatic Monologue," 374.
72 Heller, *Coleridge, Lamb, Hazlitt and the Reader of Drama*, 2, 15.
73 Jonas Barish, *The Antitheatrical Prejudice* (Berkeley: University of California Press, 1981), 343, 339; Karl Kraus, quoted in Kari Grimstad, *Masks of the Prophet: The Theatrical World of Karl Kraus* (Toronto: University of Toronto Press, 1982), v.
74 William Hazlitt, quoted in Heller, *Coleridge, Lamb, Hazlitt and the Reader of Drama*, 111. (See: William Hazlitt, *Complete Works*, ed. P. P. Howe [London: Dent, 1930], vol. 4, p. 237).
75 Charles Lamb, "On the Tragedies of Shakespeare," in *Romantic Critical Essays*, ed. David Bromwich (Cambridge, UK: Cambridge University Press, 1987), 66.
76 Ibid., 58.
77 William Hazlitt, quoted in Heller, *Coleridge, Lamb, Hazlitt and the Reader of Drama*, 105. (See: Hazlitt, *Complete Works*, vol. 4, pp. 247–248).
78 Ibid.
79 Samuel Taylor Coleridge, quoted in Heller, *Coleridge, Lamb, Hazlitt and the Reader of Drama*, 75. (See: Samuel Taylor Coleridge, *Shakespearean Criticism*, ed. Thomas Middleton Raysor [London: Constable, 1930], vol. 2, pp. 278–279.) On closet drama as standing in a dialectical relation to, rather than amounting to a simple refusal of, theatre, see Martin Puchner, *Stage Fright* (Baltimore: The Johns Hopkins University Press, 2002), 13–18.
80 It was, of course, later editors and critics, not Shakespeare, who dubbed *Hamlet* III.iv "the closet scene," but they did so on the basis of Shakespeare's own language. In IV.i Claudius recounts how "Hamlet in madness hath Polonius slain, / And from his mother's closet hath he dragged him" (William Shakespeare, *Hamlet*, ed. Sylvan Barnet [New York: Signet, 1998], IV.i.34–35, p. 95).
81 Shakespeare, *Hamlet*, III.ii.22–23, p. 68.
82 Ibid., III.iv.20–21, p. 87.
83 The situation of *a woman alone in her closet anxiously examining herself in a mirror* also occurs, as Anne Ferry has pointed out (*The "Inward" Language*

[Chicago: University of Chicago Press, 1983], 50), in the poetry of Shakespeare's contemporary, Edmund Spenser:

> One day it fortuned, faire *Britomart*
>
> Into her father's closet to repayre;
> For nothing he from her reserv'd apart,
> Being his onely daughter and his hayre [=heir]:
> Where when she had espyde that mirrhour fayre,
>
> Her selfe a while therein she vewed in vaine;
> > (*The Faerie Queene*, Book III, canto ii,
> > stanza 22, ll.1–6)

Britomart's closet, like Gertrude's, is a place very much under the sign of an absent father.

84 Richard Brathwait, *The English Gentlewoman* (1631), quoted in Straznicky, *Privacy, Playreading, and Women's Closet Drama*, 115.

85 By no one is this equivalence more emphatically asserted than Shakespeare's own Richard II, who, commanded to read out the list of accusations against him, calls for a mirror:

> I'll read enough,
> When I do see the very book indeed,
> Where all my sins are writ, and that's myself.
> > *Enter one with a glass.*
> Give me the glass, and therein will I read.

(William Shakespeare, *The Tragedy of King Richard the Second*, ed. Kenneth Muir [New York: Signet, 1963], IV.i.272–275, pp. 83–84)

86 Shakespeare, *Hamlet*, III.iv.90–91, p. 89. Certainly in later centuries a woman's "closet" came to be associated with her inner life (see Catherine B. Burroughs, *Closet Stages: Joanna Baillie and the Theater Theory of British Romantic Women Writers* [Philadelphia: University of Pennsylvania Press, 1997], 11, 177, n. 20 and Straznicky, *Privacy, Playreading, and Women's Closet Drama*, 114–116) and specifically with her acts of reading and writing, to the point where the journals, letters and diaries women produced and consumed there have themselves been characterized as "closet spaces" (Burroughs, *Closet Stages*, 31).

87 Michael Goldman, *The Actor's Freedom* (New York: Viking, 1975), 73.

88 Ibid., 107.

89 Ibid., 56.

90 Ibid., 17.

91 Ibid.

92 Ibid., 92.

93 David Cole, "Toward a Jewish Dramatic Theory," *Tikkun* 4, no. 2 (March/April 1989): 26.

94 Frances A. Yates, *Theatre of the World* (Chicago: University of Chicago Press, 1969), 182.

95 Ibid., 182, n. 24.
96 For good brief accounts of, respectively, Jerusalem Temple worship and the City Dionysia, see Lawrence Boadt, *Reading the Old Testament: An Introduction* (New York: Paulist Press, 1984), 272–285 and James H. Butler, *The Theatre and Drama of Greece and Rome* (San Francisco: Chandler, 1972), 52–55.
97 See *Leviticus* 16:2 and *First Kings* 8:6–9.
98 For this parallel between the Holy of Holies and the empty tomb, see Richard Jacobson, "Absence, Authority, and the Text," *GLYPH* 3 (1978): 146.
99 *Leviticus* 16:2.
100 *First Kings* 8:7–9.
101 For the Law as "script," see Cole, "Toward a Jewish Dramatic Theory," 26.
102 Judah Nadich, *The Legends of the Rabbis* (Northvale, NJ: Jason Aronson, 1994), vol. 1, p. 115.
103 Ibid., 72, 185.
104 Ibid., 142, 158, n. 133.
105 Ibid., 372.
106 Quoted in Samuel C. Heilman, *The People of the Book* (Chicago: University of Chicago Press, 1987), 240.
107 Ibid., 239.

Essay IV Theatre as an event and another event; or, the sorrows of realism

(Something like a manifesto)

Realistic acting, realist set and costume design, realism and naturalism, the politics of realism . . . there are, it would seem, any number of links to be drawn between realism and theatre. I shall not draw them. What follows is no patient survey or judicious critique. I have only one thing to say about realism and theatre, namely, that theatre can't (not shouldn't, but can't) be realistic because what realism wants for art is irreconcilable with how theatre works as an art.

***

Every now and then – more often than might be supposed, actually – one hears of castings like these:

- The three Cusack sisters, Sinead, Niamh and Sorcha, are cast as Chekhov's three sisters.[1]
- Brother and sister Corin and Vanessa Redgrave are cast as brother Gaev and sister Ranevskaya in *The Cherry Orchard*.[2]
- Brandon Dirden and his younger brother Jason are cast as the older and younger brothers, Lincoln and Booth, in Suzan-Lori Parks's *Topdog/ Underdog*.[3]
- Husband and wife Craig Smith and Elise Stone are cast as husband and wife Edgar and Alice in Strindberg's *Dance of Death*.[4]
- Father and son Martin and Charlie Sheen are cast as a father-and-son cop team in the film *No Code of Conduct*.[5]
- Mother and daughter Phyllida Law and Emma Thompson are cast as an aging mother and her adult daughter in the film *The Winter Guest*.[6]
- Ozzie and Harriet Nelson and their sons, Rick and David, are cast as Ozzie and Harriet Nelson and their sons, Rick and David, in the TV sitcom *The Adventures of Ozzie and Harriet*.[7]

- The Fisher family of 2004 is cast as the Fisher family of 1780 in the Grafton, Vermont Sesquicentennial Pageant.[8]
- Corrupt New Orleans politician Oliver Thomas is cast as himself in *Reflections: A Man and His Times*, a dramatization of the Oliver Thomas story.[9]

What might motivate a director to assign roles in this fashion is not hard to guess. All casting is interpretation; and castings of this type – especially when, as is often the case, the matchup between actor(s) and role(s) is close but a little "off" – carry interpretative force. When Sam West and his real-life father Timothy West play Hal *and Falstaff*,[10] the production has weighed in on the vexed question of who Hal's "real" father is. When the roles of Chekhov's three sisters are assumed by *two* sisters (Lynn and Vanessa Redgrave) and their common *niece* (Jemma Redgrave),[11] a hint is being dropped as to the quasi-parental view Olga and Masha take of Irina.

What is in it for the actors thus cast is likewise plain to see. The three Cusacks get to bring their whole rich experience of sisterhood to bear on Chekhov's trio – or perhaps to "take a break" from being the sisters they are by playing these other three. The disgraced New Orleans politician gets to portray events more his way by himself doing the portraying. And so on.

It is not, however, the actor's or director's experience of working on shows cast in this manner that interests me so much as the dilemma with which they confront an audience. Is there really all that much of a dilemma? When, for example, an (actual) mother appears as the "mother" of her (real-life) daughter, nothing would seem to hinder our describing the situation in all the terms we employ on more usual occasions. Here, too, we may say, the actor "acts (or 'plays') a part," "performs a role," "portrays (or 'feigns' or 'impersonates') a character." A production cast along these lines may, as soon as any other, be said to "stage a script" or "realize a text" or "imitate (or 'represent') an action" – as well, of course, as to offer a contrast between "illusion" (or "fiction" or "appearance") and "reality."

Now, of course, it is true that to every one of these standard terms exception has – at one time or another, on one basis or another – been taken: actors, it is urged, do not "feign" but convey inner truth; performance does not "realize" texts but is itself a text. . . . I have no dog in these fights. My aim is neither to advocate for nor to critique the traditional formulations, but merely to note that each *states a relation* (whether between actor and role, text and production, illusion and fact) and then to ask: What, if anything, might come into view if, for once, one held off from all such relational statements, not because there is anything "wrong" with them but just to see what theatre might look like in their absence? Criticism is forever seeking to make connections. How if, this once, we sought to make a *dis*connection?

Is it, however, possible to talk about theatre in other than relational terms? Actually, the oldest and most familiar of these very terms, *mimesis*, suggests that it might be:

> Tragedy . . . is an imitation of action . . . in the form of action.[12]

Something like this translation (by S. H. Butcher) of the best-known sentence from the *Poetics* has been endorsed by one after another writer on theatre. David Ross, perhaps Aristotle's most authoritative modern commentator, represents him as saying that "in drama action is imitated by action."[13] Following Ross, Francis Fergusson gives Aristotle's definition of drama as "imitation of action *in the form of action*,"[14] a phrasing quoted approvingly by Nicola Chiaromonte[15] and subsequently taken up, with variants, by more than one later critic, e.g.:

> [Mimesis] aims at situations in which actions are imitated by other actions.[16]
>
> [D]rama imitates action and . . . is symbolic action.[17]

And yet, there is an unacknowledged difficulty with all such renderings. The Greek words Butcher et al. translate as "action" are in fact two *different* Greek words. For the "action" of which tragedy is an imitation, Aristotle uses the noun, *praxis*; for the "action" by which tragedy does its imitating, he has recourse to the participle, *drōntōn*, "enacting" or "doing." True, over the course of the *Poetics*, Aristotle employs forms of these two words for "action" more or less interchangeably.[18] Nevertheless, the fact that two *different* words are being thus interchanged has implications. To say "Theatre is an action in the form of *another* [word for] action" comes very near to saying "Theatre is this action . . . *and this other*" – comes, that is, very near to undoing the very relation one set out to assert. Never mind that, a word, a beat, a gesture at a time, the two actions correspond point for point. When at the end of Act III of *The Three Sisters*, Niamh Cusack as Irina informs Sorcha Cusack as Olga that she intends to marry the Baron, two distinct things happen: (1) a character announces an intention; (2) an actress delivers a curtain line. And when we attend a performance in which the Cusack sisters play the Prozoroffs, we are throughout watching two distinct things happen: the Prozoroff girls pursue their lives together; the Cusack girls do their Chekhov together. It is customary to stress the *relation between* two such lines of action: one "stages" or "imitates" or "realizes" the other. But it is also possible to look past any such link and simply recognize that what we have before us on such occasions is *at once an event and another event*.

This, however, amounts to saying that what we have before us on such occasions is an irony, "that deep-down need to mean two things at once, to be in two places at once,"[19] that "double exposure . . . on one plate."[20] But if productions cast in this manner clearly present an irony, they would seem, no less clearly, to present a special case: the roles of the Prozoroff sisters are not normally taken by actual sisters. However, what appears a special case is really only a specially vivid instance of the general case. With three actresses sent over by their agents to play the Prozoroffs and meeting for the first time that morning, we are no less in the presence of *these* and *these others, the actors' interplay* and *the action of the play* – in short, *an event and another event*. A pointedly ironic casting – Martin and Charlie Sheen as father-and-son cops, the 2004 Fishers as the 1780 Fishers – forces the issue on our attention by forcing the issue. But, however cast, a theatre performance has the structure of an irony. We set out to ask what theatre might look like in the absence of its usual relational vocabularies: text and production, illusion and reality, performer and role.

The answer is: it looks like irony. At first glance, irony might seem just one more of the relational pairings to be jettisoned; for is not irony precisely a relation between what is said and what is meant, how it looks and how it is? But the irony of a theatre performance being at once *this* and *this other* event cannot be set aside; it is what remains after all the setting aside; it is the situation of theatre itself.

There is, to be sure, a long tradition of associating theatre with irony, but almost always on the wrong basis, for the wrong reasons.[21] Consider, for example, the familiar critical concept of "dramatic irony." From time to time, one or another critic has argued that irony is constitutive of poetry[22] or the novel.[23] Yet only theatre is commonly regarded as possessing an irony all its own, the so-called "tragic" or "Sophoclean" or, most commonly, "dramatic irony," as Bishop Thirlwell first named it in his 1833 essay "On the Irony of Sophocles."[24] Here would seem to be just such a recognition of the special ties between theatre and irony as I have been arguing for.

What, however, is actually meant by dramatic irony? "The irony occurring when the implications of a situation, speech, etc. are understood by the audience but not by the characters in the play," as when, for example, in Sophocles' *Electra*, Orestes responds to Aegisthus' order that Clytemnestra be summoned with the words "she is with you now" – meaning, her as yet veiled corpse is.[25] So understood, dramatic irony is no less present when one reads, or even reads a summary of, *Electra* than when one sees it acted. Dramatic irony, in other words, may occur in, but is scarcely limited to, theatre or even to the texts performed in theatres, and so cannot constitute the essential irony–theatre link. The connection, one senses, has been felt but not made.

We come nearer to, but still remain at a remove from, irony's true link with theatre when we consider the prominence of *conflict* there. *Why is there conflict in theatre?* is not a question it very often occurs to us to ask, any more than *why are there forms in painting* or *sounds in music?* Like forms in painting or sounds in music, conflict in theatre – whether of persons, values or styles – seems to us pretty much the nature of the thing. And so it is – but not because only the conflictual is "dramatic." (Is the *Purgatorio* any less dramatic for tracing a course from assent to deeper assent?)

"[A] play," Bert States uncontroversially holds, "must have a conflict rising to a crisis, show wills being exerted against each other, present some sort of disequilibrium."[26] True, but the clashes of will, values, etc. so characteristic of dramatic texts are really only reflections back *into* the dramatic text of the situation in which dramatic texts must at length find themselves. "Whenever we can detect some form of oppositional development, or *tendency toward contradiction*, the conditions of drama arise."[27] Yes, since the conditions of drama arise in the theatre, itself even such an "oppositional development" or "tendency toward contradiction." "Drama," States cautions, "is not conflict; it is conflict informed by ironic necessity."[28] Well, but the very structure of irony is *already* conflict – and thereby already drama. If, as the German romantic philosopher Solger thought, irony is "the true basis of all dramatic art,"[29] this is because "all dramatic art" – theatre itself – has irony's own structure of an unresolvable tension between *this* and *this other* event: the Cusacks doing their Chekhov, the Prozoroffs doing their lives.

***

None of this bodes well for the prospects of realism in the theatre.

What, it may be asked, has a possible link between theatre and irony to do with realism?

Not much, so long as by "realism" is meant no more than a concern for fidelity of depiction.

In practice, of course, realist artists rarely confine their ambition to such fidelity; they seek no less to expose conditions, foreground abuses. . . . Still, whatever other aims realism may set itself, somewhere near the top of the list must always figure what Edmund Gosse called "the exact reproduction of life,"[30] whether by "exact reproduction" is meant the deidealizing vision of Courbet, the truth-to-surfaces of 1970s photorealism, or the telling it like it is of Frank Norris and Upton Sinclair. In theatre, "exact reproduction of life" has meant everything from the "inner truth" of Stanislavskian acting to the archaeological accuracy of Meininger set design.

And yet, for all the prominence accorded it by practitioners of realism, theatrical and otherwise, fidelity of depiction has never been the true goal of realistic art so much as a running assurance that that goal is being pursued.

Most basically, realist art aspires to "represent[ ] human life without comment,"[31] "unmediated by anecdote or explanation"[32] – to "see and know all without . . . obstacle."[33] It prides itself on being "a . . . transparent style"[34] that "views [the world] through a clear glass screen."[35] Transparency might at first appear no more than a trope for accurate representation, but in fact it is a trope that leaves representation behind. With realistic artworks, "the term *representation* might be replaced by 'presentation'";[36] for what realist art claims to offer is ultimately no mere depiction, however faithful, but "life itself making an appearance"[37] (as Maupassant said of *Madame Bovary*) – the presence, glimpsed through "clear glass," of actual scenes, persons and events.

Of all the arts, theatre might seem best able to make good on this unlikely claim and so prove itself the true home of realism. With any other art, the representational means are distinct from what they would represent, and this must place bounds on that art's pretensions to convey "life itself . . . unmediated . . . without comment." Victor Hugo powerfully narrates the Battle of Waterloo,[38] but clauses are not sorties. Manet vividly paints an execution by firing squad,[39] but brushstrokes are not gunfire. In the theatre, though, when "the King rises" . . . a guy gets off a chair. This art that offers its imitations of action "in the form of action" seems likelier than most to bring you into the presence of, bring you the presence of, the event itself, being itself an event.

Of course, any such claim on theatre's part to be supplying the event itself (*startled king finds self on feet*) would appear to be undercut by its being, in fact, a different event (*prepared actor performs startled king*) that theatre at length supplies. The imitation of action is plainly by way of *another* action, as we saw acknowledged in Aristotle's employment of different terms for each. Sometimes, though, there is little enough distance between imitation and imitated that the realist boast to be setting "life itself" before us cannot so readily be dismissed.

Peter Handke's mime-play *My Foot My Tutor* consists entirely of stage directions to be executed by its two mute characters, "the warden" and "the ward." For the most part this script, when performed, is, like any script, going to produce one after another disparity of the "prepared actor/startled king" variety. For example:

> The warden extends his legs under the table.
> The ward also extends his legs under the table and comes to a halt when
>   he touches the warden's feet.[40]

It is not difficult here to distinguish "the ward's" sudden, reflexive response from the actor's deliberate playing of such a reflex. But there is at least one moment in *My Foot My Tutor* when this comfortable distinction goes by the board:

The ward eats the apple, as if no one were watching.[41]

Shall we maintain that the character bites into, chews, swallows the apple, while the actor merely *plays* biting, chewing, swallowing? Try explaining that distinction to the apple! Here, surely, for a moment, realism makes good on its claim to bring us "life itself."

Well, it is only a moment. What, though, shall we say of the following hourlong performance piece that, over its full length and by its very nature, asserts the identical claim?

TITLE: Rubbing Piece
DATE: May, 1970
MEDIUM: Performance (arm, hand, rubbing)
LOCATION: Max's Kansas City Restaurant, New York
SIZE: One hour

. . .

Activity: 1. Sitting alone at a booth, during the ordinary activity at the restaurant.
2. With my right hand, rubbing my left forearm for one hour gradually producing a sore.[42]

How can one dispute the pretensions of this 1970 "performance at the limits of performance" to be the very thing it portrays? The setting of the piece is the site specified by the piece, an actual booth in a (once) actual restaurant. The performer of the piece's actions is the performer of the piece, Vito Acconci. And the action of the piece is indistinguishable from the series of acts Mr. Acconci performs: his reddening arm could not tell you whether it is being rubbed sore in fiction or in fact. Surely here, if ever, theatrical realism attains its ambition to provide the thing itself.

And yet, it is just here, where success seems most assured, that the impossibility of any such success shows plainest. Yes, *Rubbing Piece* is indistinguishable from the actual event of a man in a booth at Max's Kansas City rubbing his arm till it hurts. But, as Kant long ago argued, "a product of fine art must be recognized to be art and not nature"[43] – must, that is, be recognized as what George Dickie calls "a candidate for appreciation by . . . the art world."[44] In the present instance, what must be recognized is that the offering of the rubbed-sore arm as "a candidate for appreciation" is *another* event than the (otherwise indistinguishable) rubbing sore of the arm. Once again, as on more commonplace occasions, theatre proves to be *an event and another event*. The two events are, as in much subsequent performance art, indistinguishable, and their being so gives rise to irony – say one thing and mean another while all the while saying only the one thing – which thus reappears as the structure of this as of the more usual sort of theatre event. Realism, "life itself," finds no place in the theatre – or rather, finds itself in the place of that irony it dreams to supplant but which, so far as theatre is concerned, is the only place to be.

Surely, though, it must prejudice the argument against theatrical realism to be always drawing one's examples from *experimental* theatre (a chafed arm in Max's Kansas City). For one thing, when theatre turns experimental, is it not, most often, from realism that it turns? And then, what about all those great realistic *plays* from . . . to . . . ? (And here the reader is free to insert his or her own canon: let's say, from *An Enemy of the People* to *Glengarry Glen Ross*.)

As with irony, my focus here is on the performance event, not dramatic texts. But as with irony,[45] the situation of realism in the theatre tends to get reflected back onto the texts performed there. If some of these texts are masterpieces, their mastery often as not consists in a masterful displacement of their own struggle with realism back onto the struggles they realistically depict.

Time and again, late in the action of a realistic play, a character will achieve a moment of vision that looks like nothing so much as an attempt *on the play's part* to see past the constraints of its own realistic mode. Here are three such moments:

SONIA: We shall live, Uncle Vanya. We'll live through a long, long line of days, endless evenings; we'll bear patiently the trials fate sends us; we'll work for others . . . and we shall rest. I have faith, I believe warmly, passionately. . . . (*Kneeling before him and putting her head on his hands; in a tired voice*) We shall rest!

(Chekhov, *Uncle Vanya*, Act 4)[46]

LENNY: This – this vision just sort of came into my mind.
BABE: A vision? What was it of?
LENNY: I don't know exactly. It was something about the three of us smiling and laughing together.
BABE: Well, when was it? Was it far away or near?
LENNY: I'm not sure; but it wasn't forever; it wasn't for every minute. Just this one moment. . . .

(Beth Henley, *Crimes of the Heart*, Act 3)[47]

ROBERT: [*In a voice which is suddenly ringing with the happiness of hope.*]
  You mustn't feel sorry for me. Don't you see I'm happy at last – free –
  free! – freed from the farm – free to wander on and on eternally! [*He
  raises himself on his elbow, his face radiant, and points to the horizon.*]
  Look! Isn't it beautiful beyond the hills? . . . It isn't the end. It's a free
  beginning – the start of my voyage . . . beyond the horizon!

(O'Neill, Beyond the Horizon, Act 3, scene 2)[48]

Ckekhov's Sonia looks ahead to a time when she and her uncle will leave
off their life of labor on others' behalf. Henley's Lenny (Lenora) foresees a
moment of shared, easy rapport with her sisters Meg and Babe, with whom,
till now, she has been mostly at odds. O'Neill's Robert envisions himself
striking free of the medical, financial and romantic pressures that all his life
have pinned him to his native place.

In each instance, however, the speaker's "vision" turns out to be not of
something above or beyond or subsequent to the play, but rather of what is
happening onstage *now*, i.e., of the speaker's present act of self-envisioning.
The "rest" Sonia predicts that she and Vanya will at last find from "the long
line of days," she even now takes, leaving off work and "putting her head on
his hands" on this first of their shared "endless evenings." The "vision" Lenny
entertains of herself and her sisters "smiling and laughing together" for "this
one moment" is a vision of *this* one moment – of Lenny's birthday party cur-
rently in progress onstage – as is acknowledged when, in the play's final stage
direction, "*the sisters freeze for a moment laughing*" and "[*t*]*he lights change
and frame them in a magical, golden, sparkling glimmer.*"[49] The "horizon"
beyond which O'Neill's dying Robert imagines himself "free to wander on . . .
eternally" is the vista his wandering mind contemplates at this very instant –
the view out his own front door. For its final vision of "what awaits," each of
these realistic plays can manage only a vision of its own act of awaiting.

This may be taken as an honest avowal on realism's part of its own inevitable limitations, a recognition that, in Wallace Stevens' words:

> the absence of the imagination had
> Itself to be imagined.[50]

But there is an irony here we should not miss, the more so as it amounts to
a return, within realism, of that very irony upon which theatre is founded
and from which realism fancies itself to have escaped. For what, after all, is
portrayed in each of these scenes but *an event* (Sonia's/Lenny's/Robert's act
of envisioning escape) and *another event* (Sonia's/Lenny's/Robert's envisioned escape) held in the ironic tension of these turning out to be, in the
end, "the same" event.

Not all realistic plays contain such a scene, but all realistic theatre must struggle to contain the tensions that such scenes play out. Theatre must fail to be realistic not because it is "really" oneiric or presentational or some other thing, but because realism, in wishing away the distance between an event and another event, wishes away theatre.

What, then, impels realists, especially in America, to try their fortunes onstage? What has realism to hope from an art by every measure so at odds with it?

In Essay II I spoke of a longing on the part of *texts* – impatient of their secondary status as mere recountings, retellings – to be *events*, and showed how, often enough, this has led texts of every sort to proclaim themselves "theatre" – theatre being, after all, the place where at least *one* kind of text (the script) routinely attains the status of (performance) event.[51]

Now, as we have seen, something very like this hankering to be an act or force or presence in the world likewise characterizes realism. The realist artwork, too, claims to be "life itself making an appearance";[52] in accounts of it as well, "the term *representation* might be replaced by 'presentation'."[53] Realist art, in other words, also aspires to event-status. What more natural, then, than for realist writers to seek out theatre, the place where texts routinely "go" to be events?

Unfortunately for realism, however, it finds in theatre one event too many; finds, that is to say, *an event and another event* locked in that ironic tension that realism had promised to dispel.

Surely, though, this cannot be the whole story on theatre's dealings with realism? Certainly some astute recent critics have proposed ampler perspectives. Amy Holzapfel,[54] for example, would avert the collapse of realism into irony by arguing that realism is less a matter of showing the world as it is than "a practice of making visible the act of seeing." But in such formulations of hers as "Ibsen's realism . . . strove to achieve an illusion of reality on the stage while simultaneously exposing the futility of such an . . . undertaking," the dismissed irony reappears. Likewise, Stanton B. Garner Jr[55] pleads for a view of "the many 'anti-realistic' practices of the twentieth century" as "in dialogue with realism." But once again, any such "dialogue," "playing out," as it must, between "contradictory modes of disclosure," seems fated to end in that intractable irony which is the life of theatre and the death of realism.

Notes

1 T. J. Binyon, "The Cry from the Provinces," *TLS* (August 3–9, 1990): 825.
2 John Stokes, "The Failing Centre Cannot Hold," *TLS* (October 6, 2000): 21.
3 Erik Piepenburg, "Dirden Brothers Cast as Brothers in 'Topdog'," *New York Times* (August 29, 2012): C2.

62   *Theatre as an event and another event*

4 See the actor bios of Smith and Stone on pp. 4–5 of the program for the Jean Cocteau Repertory production of *The Dance of Death* (New York, February 8–May 12, 2002).
5 See the synopsis of the film in *TV GUIDE* (December 9–15, 2000): 174.
6 Leah Rozen, review of *The Winter Guest*, *PEOPLE* (February 8, 1998): 22.
7 Bruce Weber, "David Nelson, Son in 'Ozzie and Harriet,' Dies at 74," *New York Times* (January 13, 2011): A23.
8 Parade Roster for the May 29, 2004 Grafton, Vermont sesquicentennial parade.
9 Campbell Robertson, "Lead Plays Himself in Drama on Scandal," *New York Times* (January 14, 2011): A12.
10 The Wests, father and son, appeared together in the Royal Shakespeare Company's 1997 production of *Henry IV*. See photo and caption in the *TLS* (May 4, 2001): 5.
11 See the weekly theatre listings for December 17–26, 1990 in the *New Yorker* (December 24, 1990): 4, and the photo of the three Redgraves, aunts and niece, in *PEOPLE* (December 24, 1990): 61.
12 Aristotle, *Poetics*, trans. S. H. Butcher (New York: Dover, 1951), 23.
13 David Ross, *Aristotle* (London: Methuen, 1971), 280.
14 Francis Fergusson, *The Idea of a Theater* (New York: Doubleday, 1949), 23 (italics in original). Fergusson also supplied the introduction to a 1961 reprint of Butcher's translation of the *Poetics*, in which he again quotes the sentence in question in Butcher's version. See Francis Fergusson, Introduction to Aristotle, *Poetics*, trans. S. H. Butcher (New York: Hill and Wang, 1961), 7.
15 Nicola Chiaromonte, *The Worm of Consciousness* (New York: Harcourt Brace Jovanovich, 1976), 101.
16 Gunter Gebauer and Christoph Wulf, *Mimesis: Culture, Art, Society* (Berkeley: University of California Press, 1995), 55.
17 John D. Boyd, *The Function of Mimesis and Its Decline* (Cambridge, MA: Harvard University Press, 1968), 55.
18 John Jones, *On Aristotle and Greek Tragedy* (Stanford: Stanford University Press, 1962), 59. The forms thus interchangeably employed by Aristotle are *prattontes* and *drōntes*, "enacters" and "doers," respectively, in Jones's translation. See the passages from the *Poetics* cited by Jones on 59, n. 1.
19 Edward St. Aubyn, quoted in Laura Kipnis, "I Mean It," *New York Times Book Review* (August 12, 2012): 17.
20 Allan Rodway, quoted in D. C. Muecke, *The Compass of Irony* (London: Methuen, 1969), 29.
21 For a brief account of this tradition, see Marvin Carlson, *The Haunted Stage* (Ann Arbor: University of Michigan Press, 2001), 28–29, and references there.
22 This was the position of the New Critics I. A. Richards and Cleanth Brooks.
23 Thus for the Marxist critic Georg Lukács "irony . . . is the normative mentality of the novel." (Georg Lukács, *The Theory of the Novel* [Cambridge, MA: MIT Press, 1983], 84).
24 G. G. Sedgewick, *Of Irony, Especially in Drama* (Toronto: University of Toronto Press, 1935), 20, 23.
25 www.dictionary.com/browse/dramatic-irony. The Sophoclean example (*Electra*, l. 1474) is cited in Muecke, *Compass of Irony*, 106.
26 Bert O. States, *Irony and Drama* (Ithaca: Cornell University Press, 1971), 15.
27 Ibid., 14 (italics in original).
28 Ibid., 24.

29 Karl Wilhelm Ferdinand Solger, quoted in Søren Kierkegaard, *The Concept of Irony*, trans. Lee M. Capel (Bloomington: Indiana University Press, 1968), 261n.
30 Edmund Gosse, "The Limits of Realism in Fiction," in *Documents of Modern Realism*, ed. George J. Becker (Princeton: Princeton University Press, 1963), 389.
31 Northrop Frye, *Anatomy of Criticism* (New York: Atheneum, 1969), 285.
32 Linda Nochlin, *Realism* (New York: Penguin, 1979), 167. Nochlin is commenting on Manet's painting, "At the Café."
33 Elin Diamond, *Unmasking Mimesis* (London: Routledge, 1997), 51.
34 Nochlin, *Realism*, 14.
35 Peter Brooks, *Realist Vision* (New Haven: Yale University Press, 2005), 125.
36 Ibid., 86. Brooks is discussing the effect of early photographs.
37 Guy de Maupassant, quoted in Becker, *Documents*, 89.
38 Victor Hugo, *Les Misérables*, trans. Lee Fahnestock and Norman MacAfee (New York: Penguin, 1987), "Cosette," Book One, Chapter 1, "Waterloo," 301–358.
39 Édouard Manet, "The Execution of the Emperor Maximillian," reproduced in Nochlin, *Realism*, 30.
40 Peter Handke, "My Foot My Tutor," in *The Ride Across Lake Constance and Other Plays*, trans. Michael Roloff (New York: Farrar, Straus and Giroux, 1976), 36.
41 Handke, "My Foot My Tutor," 31. For this and the Vito Acconci example discussed below I am indebted to two articles by Michael Kirby in *The Drama Review* 16, no. 1 (T-53; March 1972): "On Acting and Not-Acting," 3–15 and "Performance at the Limits of Performance," 70–71.
42 Vito Acconci, "Rubbing Piece," *The Drama Review* 16, no. 1 (T-53; March 1972): 72.
43 Immanuel Kant, *Critique of Judgement*, trans. James Creed Meredith (Oxford: Oxford University Press, 1978), Part I, para. 45, p. 166.
44 George Dickie, *Art and the Aesthetic* (Ithaca: Cornell University Press, 1974), 34.
45 See above, Essay IV, pp. 55–56.
46 Anton Chekhov, "Uncle Vanya," in *Best Plays*, trans. Stark Young (New York: Random House, 1956), act 4, pp. 134–135.
47 Beth Henley, *Crimes of the Heart* (New York: Penguin, 1982), act 3, pp. 122–123.
48 Eugene O'Neill, "Beyond the Horizon," in *Early Plays*, ed. Jeffrey H. Richards (New York: Penguin, 2001), act 3, scene 2, p. 193.
49 Henley, *Crimes of the Heart*, act 3, p. 125sd.
50 Wallace Stevens, "The Plain Sense of Things," ll. 13–14, in *Collected Poems* (New York: Knopf, 1969), 503.
51 See Essay II, p. 16.
52 See Essay IV, n. 37.
53 See Essay IV, n. 36.
54 Amy Holzapfel, *Art, Vision and Nineteenth-Century Realist Drama* (New York: Routledge, 2014), 186, 82.
55 Stanton B. Garner Jr, "Sensing Realism: Illusionism, Actuality, and the Theatrical Sensorium," in *The Senses in Performance*, ed. Sally Banes and André Lepecki (New York: Routledge, 2007), 115–122.

Words for the theatre

*Theatre dreams of persuading writing
to come forth and be for the event – be
utterance, be action! Yet it is only by abiding,
musingly, within itself that writing can be
an event for theatre. What is theatre but
the spectacle of writing keeping dramatically
to itself?*

*Writing refuses itself to theatre, and theatre
goes on to stage the refusal – is, indeed, best
understood as the staging of this refusal.*

*Writing is a Muse that would have absolutely
nothing to say to theatre, did not theatre draw
endless inspiration from the spectacle of a Muse
with nothing to say to it.*

*Theatre will not be dictated to by writing,
but may come to find, in the scene of dictation
it foregoes, the text it desires.*

Index

Acconci, Vito 58–59
Anouilh, Jean 1
Anselm, St. 3
Aristotle 54

Barthes, Roland 39–40
Bentley, Eric 1, 8n4
Berkeley, George 3
Berrigan, Daniel 1
Boccaccio, Giovanni 6–7
Book of Common Prayer 6
books as "theatres" 13–14, 16–17, 19, 26–27
Brecht, Bertolt ix, 6, 43
Brook, Peter 2–3
Burton, Robert 35

Camillo, Giulio 38–39, 40
Carlson, Marvin 2, 62n21
casting: as interpretation 53; ironies of 52–53, 55
Chekhov, Anton 52–53, 59–60
City Dionysia 44
closet drama 3–4, 36, 42–43; closet scene in *Hamlet* as prototype of 43; and solitary reading 42–43; and women's inner lives 50n86
Cole, David 10n15, 41
Cole, Toby ix
Coleridge, Samuel Taylor 42
conflict 56; irony as basis of 56

de Man, Paul 14–15
Dickens, Charles 18, 37
Dickie, George 58

Dickinson, Emily 37, 38
dramatic monologues 41–42
dramatic text as theatre "gone in" 41–46
dramatourgos (= "playwright") viii–ix
dramaturg-playwright relation viii–ix, xii
Dryden, John 3, 42

event: dramatic text as future 16, 26–27, 28, 61; painting as 15; poem as x, 14, 17; prose fiction as 14, 17–18; text as x, 14–18, 20, 61; *see also* theatre event
"event and another event" (theatre as) 54–55, 59, 60, 61

Faulkner, William 24–26
Fornes, Maria Irene 1
Freud, Sigmund 34, 35
Frost, Robert 15, 17

Garner, Stanton B., Jr 61
Goldman, Michael 43
Gosse, Edmund 56
Greenberg, Clement 15
Grotowski, Jerzy 19

Hamilton, Emma 42
Handke, Peter 3, 57–58
Hazlitt, William 2, 9n14, 4, 42
Henley, Beth 59–60
Hollander, Anne 40
Holzapfel, Amy 61
Hugo, Victor 34
Hume, David 3, 38, 39–40, 48n55